the Best of SUCCESS

A
Treasury of
Success Ideas

compiled by

WYNN
DAVIS

Great Quotations Publishing Company
Lombard, Illinois • *a division of GREAT QUOTATIONS, INCORPORATED*

ACKNOWLEDGEMENTS

with special thanks to:
Maggie Abel
Bill Mayo
Jennifer Sekerak
Cherese Sekerak
Flo Griesinger
Greg Brendon
and
Laura Lavelle

credits

compiled and edited by: Wynn Davis
designed by: The McKee Anderson Group
art director: Peter T. Secker
calligraphy: Timothy R. Botts
production: Paul Rubens

THE BEST OF SUCCESS

ISBN: 0-931089-25-5

FIRST PRINTING, May 1988
SECOND PRINTING, September 1988
THIRD PRINTING, January 1989

C O N T E N T S

to my parents

P R E F A C E

This book grew from a simple idea: that all self-help books contain a few powerful core ideas that can be condensed into a set of success laws.

These core ideas have now been collected. So simple are these success ideas that they can almost always be expressed in one word.

Some self-help books might focus on one or two success laws, others might contain 20 or more. But never does the list appear close to being complete. And, almost always, these laws or principles of success are left partially hidden; never being fully identified.

This book is different. Each chapter contains an important idea fully identified in one or two words, explained in a few sentences, and then expanded and clarified by supporting quotations from the best success literature.

This book is a new dimension in success literature. It is a reference book, a sourcebook—a compendium of the most important success ideas.

While these ideas are simple, they are also powerful. Do not let their simplicity fool you. These are the same ideas which have made the famous, famous, and the rich, rich.

So here are ideas of fine gold. Here are the rubies, emeralds, diamonds. Here are the ultimates spread out before you to enjoy. You have now found the Best of Success.

Wynn Davis

"There are single thoughts that contain the essence of a whole volume, single sentences that have the beauties of a large work. "

JOSEPH JOUBERT

We achieve to the degree that
we overcome the negative.
Achievers are willing to pay
the price of achievement.
They sacrifice, struggle, work
on, perhaps alone, weary, and
discouraged, and yet at each
step overcome the negative.

Overcoming the negative is the
price of achievement—the
price of greatness.

Achievement

No pains, no gains.

Proverb quoted by
SAMUEL SMILES

There are no gains without pains.

BENJAMIN FRANKLIN

You've got to go through the negative before you can get to the positive.

WILLARD L. BURSON

There is no success without hardship.

SOPHOCLES

All things are difficult before they are easy.

THOMAS FULLER

I have learned that success is to be measured not so much by the position that one has reached in life as by the obstacles which he has overcome while trying to succeed.

BOOKER T. WASHINGTON

Success is not measured by what a man accomplishes, but by the opposition he has encountered, and the courage with which he has maintained the struggle against overwhelming odds. . . .

ORISON SWETT MARDEN

The honor of the conquest is rated by the difficulty.

BARON DE MONTESQUIEU

The measure of a man is the way he bears up under misfortune.

PLUTARCH

The greater the obstacle, the more glory in overcoming it.

JEAN BAPTISTE MOLIÉRE

The harder the conflict, the more glorious the triumph.

THOMAS PAINE

To win without risk is to triumph without glory.

PIERRE CORNEILLE

No pain, no palm; no thorns, no throne; no gall, no glory; no cross, no crown.

WILLIAM PENN

It is certain that the greatest poets, orators, statesmen, and historians, men of the most brilliant and imposing talents, have labored as hard, if not harder, than day laborers; and that the most obvious reason why they have been superior to other men is that they have taken more pains than other men.

ORISON SWETT MARDEN

The world is so constructed, that if you wish to enjoy its pleasures, you must also endure its pains. Whether you like it or not, you cannot have one without the other.

SWAMI BRAHMANANDA

It is not ease, but effort—not facility, but difficulty, that makes men. There is, perhaps, no station in life in which difficulties have not to be encountered and overcome before any decided measure of success can be achieved.

SAMUEL SMILES

Achievement

The battle of life is, in most cases, fought uphill; and to win it without a struggle were perhaps to win it without honour. If there were no difficulties there would be no success; if there were nothing to struggle for, there would be nothing to be achieved.

SAMUEL SMILES

He who would accomplish little must sacrifice little; he who would achieve much must sacrifice much....

JAMES ALLEN

You make up your mind before you start that sacrifice is part of the package.

RICHARD M. DeVOS

The most important thing in life is not the triumph but the struggle. The essential thing is not to have conquered but to have fought well.

BARON PIERRE DE COUBERTIN

To him that overcometh will I grant to sit with me in my throne, even as I also overcame, and am set down with my Father in his throne.

Bible, REVELATION 3:21

We gain the advantage in any situation through one medium: time. We gain the advantage by doing things before they need to be done—positioning ourselves ahead of time in the best place. Those who think ahead of the

approaching action will have the advantage. They will be the winners.

The time to repair the roof is when the sun is shining.

JOHN F. KENNEDY

In life, as in chess, forethought wins.

CHARLES BUXTON

If we do what is necessary, all the odds are in our favor.

HENRY KISSINGER

Keeping a little ahead of conditions is one of the secrets of business....

CHARLES M. SCHWAB

Do the next thing.

JOHN WANAMAKER

The wise man avoids evil by anticipating it.

PUBLILIUS SYRUS

Let our advance worrying become advance thinking and planning.

WINSTON CHURCHILL

Our attitude is not determined by circumstances, but by how we respond to circumstances. Our minds determine our attitude. We

can respond positively or negatively. It's how we react to events, not the events themselves, that determines our attitude.

Attitude

It's not the situation....It's your reaction to the situation.

BOB CONKLIN

Your living is determined not so much by what life brings to you as by the attitude you bring to life; not so much by what happens to you as by the way your mind looks at what happens.

JOHN HOMER MILLER

An obvious fact about negative feelings is often overlooked. They are caused by us, not by exterior happenings. An outside event presents the challenge, but we react to it. So we must attend to the way we take things, not to the things themselves.

VERNON HOWARD

A man is not hurt so much by what happens, as by his opinion of what happens.

MICHEL EYQUEM DE MONTAIGNE

What happens to a man is less significant than what happens within him.

LOUIS L. MANN

Any fact facing us is not as important as our attitude toward it, for that determines our success or failure.

NORMAN VINCENT PEALE

There are two big forces at work, external and internal. We have very little control over external forces such as tornados, earthquakes, floods, disasters, illness and pain. What really matters is the internal force. How do I respond to those disasters? Over that I have complete control.

LEO BUSCAGLIA

Experience is not what happens to a man; it is what a man does with what happens to him.

ALDOUS HUXLEY

It is the way we react to circumstances that determines our feeling.

DALE CARNEGIE

No one on earth can hurt you, unless you accept the hurt in your own mind....The problem is not other people; it is your reaction.

VERNON HOWARD

No one can make you feel inferior without your consent.

ELEANOR ROOSEVELT

Men are disturbed, not by the things that happen, but by their opinion of the things that happen.

EPICTETUS

You may be dead broke and that's a reality, but in spirit you may be brimming over with optimism, joy, and energy. The reality of your life may result from many outside factors, none of which you can control. Your attitudes, however, reflect the ways in which you evaluate what is happening.

H. STANLEY JUDD

I've never been poor, only broke. Being poor is a frame of mind. Being broke is only a temporary situation.

MIKE TODD

Life at any time can become difficult: life at any time can become easy. It all depends upon how one adjusts oneself to life.

MORARJI DESAI

Attitude

You cannot always control circumstances. But you can control your own thoughts.

CHARLES E. POPPLESTONE

The good or bad is not in the circumstance, but only in the mind of him that encounters it.

JAMES ALLEN

There is nothing either good or bad, but thinking makes it so.

WILLIAM SHAKESPEARE

The key to most difficulties does not lie in the dilemmas themselves, but in our relation to them.

DAVID SEABURY

It is not the position but the disposition.

J. E. DINGER

Positive thinking is reacting positively to a negative situation.

BILL HAVENS

Things turn out best for the people who make the best of the way things turn out.

JOHN WOODEN

Like the waves of the sea are the ways of fate as we voyage thru life.
'Tis the set of the soul which decides its goal and not the calm or the strife.

ELLA WHEELER WILCOX

This is the law of averages:
the more we fail, the greater
our chance of succeeding.
Failure is often the first
necessary step toward
success. And if we don't
take the risk of failing, we

won't get the chance to
succeed. When we are
trying, we are winning.

Averages

Failure is, in a sense, the highway to success....

JOHN KEATS

Mistakes are merely steps up the ladder....

PAUL J. MEYER

Some defeats are only installments to victory.

JACOB A. RIIS

Many a one has finally succeeded only because he has failed after repeated efforts. If he had never met defeat he would never have known any great victory.

ORISON SWETT MARDEN

The men who try to do something and fail are infinitely better than those who try to do nothing and succeed.

LLOYD JONES

The man who makes no mistakes does not usually make anything.

WILLIAM CONNOR MAGEE

I am not judged by the number of times I fail, but by the number of times I succeed; and the number of times I succeed is in direct proportion to the number of times I can fail and keep on trying.

TOM HOPKINS

To begin to think with purpose, is to enter the ranks of those strong ones who only recognize failure as one of the pathways to attainment....

JAMES ALLEN

Every failure is a step to success....

WILLIAM WHEWELL

Not doing more than the average is what keeps the average down.

WILLIAM M. WINANS

The success always has a number of projects planned, to which he looks forward. Any one of them could change the course of his life overnight.

MARK CAINE

The boy who is going to make a great man...must not make up his mind not merely to overcome a thousand obstacles, but to win in spite of a thousand repulses and defeats.

THEODORE ROOSEVELT

What is defeat? Nothing but education, nothing but the first step to something better.

WENDELL PHILLIPS

We learn wisdom from failure much more than from success. We often discover what will do, by finding out what will not do; and probably he who never made a mistake never made a discovery.

SAMUEL SMILES

It is a mistake to suppose that men succeed through success; they much oftener succeed through failures...Precept, study, advice, and example could never have taught them so well as failure has done.

SAMUEL SMILES

Averages

I am not discouraged, because every wrong attempt discarded is another step forward.

THOMAS A. EDISON

Mistakes are stepping stones to success.

CHARLES E. POPPLESTONE

Losing is a form of winning.

AL SCHNEIDER

Losing is a part of winning.

DICK MUNRO

You can't be a winner and be afraid to lose.

CHARLES A. LYNCH

It doesn't matter how many times you have failed...What matters is the successful attempt...

MAWELL MALTZ

I never see failure as failure, but only as the game I must play to win.

TOM HOPKINS

To win...you've got to stay in the game....

CLAUDE M. BRISTOL

Would you like me to give you a formula for...success? It's quite simple, really. Double your rate of failure.... You're thinking of failure as the enemy of success. But it isn't at all....You can be discouraged by failure—or you can learn from it. So go ahead and make mistakes. Make all you can. Because, remember that's where you'll find success. On the far side of failure.

THOMAS J. WATSON

Belief is the knowledge that we
can do something. It's the
inner feeling that what we
undertake, we can accomplish.
For the most part, all of us
have the ability to look at
something and to know

whether or not we can do it.
So in belief, there is power:
our eyes are opened;
our opportunities become plain;
our visions become realities.

Belief

Everything is possible for him who believes.

Bible, MARK 9:23

He can who thinks he can, and he can't who thinks he can't. This is an inexorable, indisputable law.

ORISON SWETT MARDEN

You can do what you think you can do and you cannot do what you think you cannot do.

BEN STEIN

If you believe you can do a thing, you can do it.

CLAUDE M. BRISTOL

Whether you think you can or think you can't—you are right.

HENRY FORD

There is no law by which one can as long as he thinks he can't.

ORISON SWETT MARDEN

In order to succeed we must first believe that we can.

MICHAEL KORDA

They can conquer who believe they can.

JOHN DRYDEN

They can...because they think they can.

VIRGIL

I found that I could find the energy...that I could find the determination to keep on going. I learned that your mind can amaze your body, if you just keep telling yourself, I can do it...I can do it...I can do it!

JON ERICKSON

A person under the firm persuasion that he can command resources virtually has them.

LIVY

When you believe you can—you can!

MAXWELL MALTZ

In the moment that you carry this conviction...in that moment your dream will become a reality.

ROBERT COLLIER

Your belief that you can do the thing gives your thought forces their power.

ROBERT COLLIER

What a thing is is to an unknowable extent determined by or influenced by what we think it is.

JOSEPH CHILTON PEARCE

You have a remarkable ability which you never acknowledged before. It is to look at a situation and know whether you can do it. And I mean really know the answer....

CARL FREDERICK

The only thing that stands between a man and what he wants from life is often merely the will to try it and the faith to believe that it is possible.

RICHARD M. DeVOS

Belief

There is nothing on earth you cannot have—once you have mentally accepted the fact that you can have it.

ROBERT COLLIER

Once you are able to make your request in such a way that you will be quite certain of its fulfillment, then the fulfillment will come.

HERMANN HESSE

The first and most important step toward...success is the feeling that we can succeed.

NELSON BOSWELL

Your chances of success in any undertaking can always be measured by your belief in yourself.

ROBERT COLLIER

We can never succeed until we believe we'll succeed.

KEITH DeGREEN

The strongest single factor in prosperity consciousness is self-esteem: believing you can do it, believing you deserve it, believing you will get it.

JERRY GILLIES

You can do anything you think you can. This knowledge is literally the gift of the gods, for through it you can solve every human problem. It should make of you an incurable optimist. It is the open door....

ROBERT COLLIER

What the mind of man can conceive and believe, the mind of a man can achieve.

NAPOLEON HILL

Our self-image prescribes the limits for the accomplishment of any particular goals. It prescribes the "area of the possible."

MAXWELL MALTZ

The mind is the limit. As long as the mind can envision the fact that you can do something, you can do it—as long as you really believe 100 percent.

ARNOLD SCHWARZENEGGER

The feeling must come first. If you actually feel rich, if you have a deep inner conviction that you will always have all that you need, it will be so.

DONALD CURTIS

It is the mind that maketh good of ill, that maketh wretch or happy, rich or poor.

EDMUND SPENSER

Success is a state of mind. If you want success, start thinking of yourself as a success.

JOYCE BROTHERS

What we sincerely believe regarding ourselves is true for us.

ORISON SWETT MARDEN

What you believe yourself to be, you are.

CLAUDE M. BRISTOL

A man is literally what he thinks.

JAMES ALLEN

Man is what he believes.

ANTON CHEKHOV

Belief

For as he thinketh in his heart, so is he.

Bible, PROVERBS 23:7

If you see yourself as prosperous, you will be. If you see yourself as continually hard up, that is exactly what you will be.

ROBERT COLLIER

We are what we think.
All that we are arises
With our thoughts.
With our thoughts,
We make our world.

GAUTAMA BUDDHA

You have to believe in yourself. And you have to, down deep within the bottom of your soul, feel that you can do the job that you've set out to do.

WILLIAM CASTLE DeVRIES

The only limit to our realization of tomorrow will be our doubts of today.

FRANKLIN DELANO ROOSEVELT

The barrier between...success is not something which exists in the real world: it is composed purely and simply of...doubts about...ability.

MARK CAINE

We clothe events with the drapery of our own thoughts....

JAMES ALLEN

These, then, are my last words to you: Be not afraid of life. Believe that life is worth living and your belief will help create the fact.

WILLIAM JAMES

Our greatest power is the
power to choose. We can decide
where we are, what we do, and

what we think. No one can
take the power to choose away
from us. It is ours alone. We
can do what we want to do.
We can be who we want to be.

Choice

You are searching for the magic key that will unlock the door to the source of power; and yet you have the key in your own hands, and you may make use of it the moment you learn to control your thoughts.

NAPOLEON HILL

Knowing that you have complete control of your thinking you will recognize the power....

MIKHAIL STRABO

The key to your universe is that you can choose.

CARL FREDERICK

The greatest power that a person possesses is the power to choose.

J. MARTIN KOHE

You can at any time decide to alter the course of your life—no one can take that away. Any person can choose to activate real directions of the self. It is true for every individual that at any moment he can choose to become himself.

CLARK MOUSTAKAS

Everything can be taken from a man but one thing: the last of the human freedoms—to choose one's attitude in any given set of circumstances, to choose one's own way.

VIKTOR E. FRANKL

We fail to see that we can control our own destiny; make ourselves do whatever is possible; make ourselves become whatever we long to be.

ORISON SWETT MARDEN

The one thing over which you have absolute control is your own thoughts. It is this that puts you in a position to control your own destiny.

PAUL G. THOMAS

The greatest discovery of my generation is that human beings can alter their lives by altering their attitudes of mind.

WILLIAM JAMES

Nature is at work. Character and destiny are her handiwork. She gives us love and hate, jealousy and reverence. All that is ours is the power to choose which impulse we shall follow.

DAVID SEABURY

You need only choose...then keep choosing as many times as necessary. That is all you need do. And it is certainly something you can do. Then as you continue to choose, everything is yours....

VERNON HOWARD

You don't have to buy from anyone. You don't have to work at any particular job. You don't have to participate in any given relationship. You can choose.

HARRY BROWNE

Though our character is formed by circumstances, our own desires can do much to shape those circumstances; and what is really inspiriting and ennobling in the doctrine of free will is the conviction that we have real power over the formation of our own character....

JOHN STUART MILL

You can do what you want to do. You can be what you want to be.

R. DAVID THOMAS

Choice

You always do what you want to do. This is true with every act. You may say that you had to do something, or that you were forced to, but actually, whatever you do, you do by choice. Only you have the power to choose for yourself.

W. CLEMENT STONE

I am the master of my fate;
I am the captain of my soul.

WILLIAM ERNEST HENLEY

We stand at the helm and know that we are masters of our fate and not its slave—master of our joys and master of our sorrows.

HANS-ULRICH RIEKER

A man sooner or later discovers that he is the master-gardener of his soul, the director of his life.

JAMES ALLEN

There's no feeling quite like the one you get when you get to the truth: You're the captain of the ship called you. You're setting the course, the speed, and you're out there on the bridge, steering.

CARL FREDERICK

The choice is yours. You hold the tiller. You can steer the course you choose in the direction of where you want to be—today, tomorrow, or in a distant time to come.

W. CLEMENT STONE

It is always your next move.

NAPOLEON HILL

We can know what people are thinking by looking at what they do. Actions mirror thoughts. And by taking a good look at where we are and what we are doing, we can understand what we are

thinking. The thoughts we have chosen have brought us where we are today.

Circumstance

Man's mind is his essence; he is where his thoughts are.

NAHMAN OF BRATZLAV

Every man is where he is by the law of his being; the thoughts which he has built into his character have brought him there.

JAMES ALLEN

You are where you are today because you've chosen to be there.

HARRY BROWNE

We are exactly where we have chosen to be.

VERNON HOWARD

People are where they are because that's exactly where they really want to be...whether they'll admit that or not.

EARL NIGHTINGALE

That we are here is proof that we ought to be here.

RALPH WALDO EMERSON

How things look on the outside of us depends on how things are on the inside of us.

PARKS COUSINS

Invariably it is true—as is the inner so always and inevitably will be the outer.

RALPH WALDO TRINE

It is a fact that you project what you are.

NORMAN VINCENT PEALE

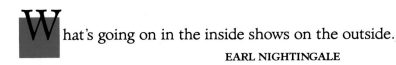What's going on in the inside shows on the outside.

EARL NIGHTINGALE

How we think shows through in how we act. Attitudes are mirrors of the mind. They reflect thinking.

DAVID JOSEPH SCHWARTZ

A man's action is only a picture book of his creed.

RALPH WALDO EMERSON

As I grow older, I pay less attention to what men say. I just watch what they do.

ANDREW CARNEGIE

The lectures you deliver may be wise and true, But I'd rather get my lessons by observing what you do. I may not understand the high advise you like to give, But there's no misunderstanding how you act and how you live.

EDGAR A. GUEST

You can preach a better sermon with your life than with your lips.

OLIVER GOLDSMITH

The finest eloquence is that which gets things done.

DAVID LLOYD GEORGE

He does not believe that does not live according to his belief.

THOMAS FULLER

Behavior is the perpetual revealing of us. What a man does, tells us what he is.

F. D. HUNTINGTON

Circumstance

The actions of men are the best interpreters of their thoughts.

JOHN LOCKE

Action will remove the doubt that theory cannot solve.

TEHYI HSIEH

You will know them by their fruits.

Bible, MATTHEW 7:16

A man bears beliefs, as a tree bears apples.

RALPH WALDO EMERSON

They do not love that do not show their love.

JOHN HEYWOOD

By the work one knows the workman.

JEAN DE LA FONTAINE

This is the law of compensation: Every negative has a positive. We cannot have

the bad without the good. With every loss comes a gain. And within every difficulty, there's an opportunity. Seeing success where others see only failure may be the one thing that pushes us on to victory.

Compensation

For every force, there is a counterforce. For every negative there is a positive. For every action there is a reaction. For every cause there is an effect.

GRACE SPEARE

To every action there is always opposed an equal reaction....

SIR ISAAC NEWTON

There must be a positive and negative in everything in the universe in order to complete a circuit or circle, without which there would be no activity, no motion.

JOHN McDONALD

Polarity, or action and reaction, we meet in every part of nature; in darkness and light; in heat and cold; in the ebb and flow of waters; in male and female; in the inspiration and expiration of plants and animals; in the equation of quantity and quality, in the fluids of the animal body; in the systole and diastole of the heart.

RALPH WALDO EMERSON

For everything you have missed, you have gained something else; and for everything you gain, you lose something else.

RALPH WALDO EMERSON

Did you think you could have the good without the evil? Did you think you could have the joy without the sorrow?

DAVID GRAYSON

There are no...great gains without some losses, no goods without some evils, no winning without some failing.

DAVID SEABURY

You cannot have the success without the failures.

H. G. HASLER

Prosperity is not without many fears and distastes; and adversity is not without comforts and hopes.

FRANCIS BACON

Every failure brings with it the seed of an equivalent success.

NAPOLEON HILL

In every adversity there lies the seed of an equivalent advantage. In every defeat there is a lesson showing you how to win the victory next time.

ROBERT COLLIER·

There is a good side to every situation....

DAVID JOSEPH SCHWARTZ

Every crucial experience can be regarded as a setback—or the start of a new kind of development.

MARY ROBERTS RINEHART

Any experience can be transformed into something of value.

VASH YOUNG

I always tried to turn every disaster into an opportunity.

JOHN D. ROCKEFELLER

Consider every mistake you do make as an asset.

PAUL J. MEYER

Compensation

Even a mistake may turn out to be the one thing necessary to a worthwhile achievement.

HENRY FORD

There are occasions when it is undoubtedly better to incur loss than to make gain.

PLAUTUS

A stumble may prevent a fall.

THOMAS FULLER

What looks like a loss may be the very event which is subsequently responsible for helping to produce the major achievements of your life.

SRULLY BLOTNICK

Never walk away from failure. On the contrary, study it carefully—and imaginatively—for its hidden assets.

MICHAEL KORDA

All my successes have been built on my failures.

BENJAMIN DISRAELI

Sweet are the uses of adversity; which, like the toad, ugly and venomous, wears yet a precious jewel in his head.

WILLIAM SHAKESPEARE

Everything depends upon the way we look at things.

ORISON SWETT MARDEN

The hopeful man sees success where others see failure, sunshine where others see shadows and storm.

ORISON SWETT MARDEN

To know how to wring victory from defeat, and make stepping-stones of our stumbling-blocks, is the secret of success.

ORISON SWETT MARDEN

One has to remember that every failure can be a stepping-stone to something better....

COLONEL HARLAND SANDERS

What are stumbling blocks and defeat to the weak and vacillating are but stepping-stones to victory to the determined soul.

ORISON SWETT MARDEN

Develop success from failures. Discouragement and failure are two of the surest stepping stones to success. No other element can do so much for a man if he is willing to study them and make capital out of them.

DALE CARNEGIE

The pessimist sees the difficulty in every opportunity. The optimist, the opportunity in every difficulty.

L. P. JACKS

An optimist sees an opportunity in every calamity; a pessimist sees a calamity in every opportunity.

WINSTON CHURCHILL

The optimist sees the doughnut, the pessimist, the hole.

McLANDBURGH WILSON

Two men look out through the same bars:
One sees the mud, and one the stars.

FREDERICK LANGBRIDGE

Compensation

When it is dark enough you can see the stars.

RALPH WALDO EMERSON

We must look for the opportunity in every difficulty instead of being paralyzed at the thought of the difficulty in every opportunity.

WALTER E. COLE

View every problem as an opportunity....

JOSEPH SUGARMAN

Try to regard every problem that comes your way as opportunity rather than opposition, as opulence rather than oppression.

RUSSELL J. FORNWALL

When difficulties confront you, baptize them opportunity and set the man inside you to finding the way to turn them from difficulties into opportunities.

ROBERT COLLIER

There is no such thing as a problem without a gift.... You seek problems because you need their gifts.

RICHARD BACH

Every problem has in it the seeds of its own solution. If you don't have any problems, you don't get any seeds....

NORMAN VINCENT PEALE

Welcome every problem as an opportunity. Each moment is the greatest challenge, the best thing that ever happened to you. The more difficult the problem, the greater the challenge in working it out.

GRACE SPEARE

Concentration is the magic key that opens the door to accomplishment. By concentrating our efforts upon a few major goals, our efficiency soars, our projects are completed—we are going somewhere. By focusing our

efforts to a single point, we achieve the greatest results.

Concentration

Concentration is my motto—first honesty, then industry, then concentration.

ANDREW CARNEGIE

The first rule of success, and the one that supersedes all others, is to have energy. It is important to know how to concentrate it, how to husband it, how to focus it on important things instead of frittering it away on trivia.

MICHAEL KORDA

Singleness of purpose is one of the chief essentials for success in life, no matter what may be one's aim.

JOHN D. ROCKEFELLER, JR.

The first law of success...is concentration—to bend all the energies to one point, and to go directly to that point, looking neither to the right nor to the left.

WILLIAM MATHEWS

I never could have done what I have done without the habits of punctuality, order, and diligence, without the determination to concentrate myself on one subject at a time....

CHARLES DICKENS

Success....My nomination for the single most important ingredient is energy well directed.

LOUIS B. LUNDBORG

Every great man has become great, every successful man has succeeded, in proportion as he has confined his powers to one particular channel.

ORISON SWETT MARDEN

The giants of the race have been men of concentration, who have struck sledge-hammer blows in one place until they have accomplished their purpose. The successful men of today are men of one overmastering idea, one unwavering aim, men of single and intense purpose.

ORISON SWETT MARDEN

This is an age of organized effort. On every hand we see evidence that organization is the basis of all financial success, and while other factors than that of organization enter into the attainment of success, this factor is still one of major importance.

NAPOLEON HILL

Concentration is the key to economic results...no other principle of effectiveness is violated as constantly today as the basic principle of concentration....Our motto seems to be: "Let's do a little bit of everything."

PETER F. DRUCKER

The man who succeeds above his fellows is the one who early in life clearly discerns his object, and towards that object habitually directs his powers.

EDWARD GEORGE BULWER-LYTTON

Any individual can be, in time, what he earnestly desires to be, if he but set his face steadfastly in the direction of that one thing and bring all his powers to bear upon its attainment.

J. HERMAN RANDALL

The ability to apply your physical and mental energies to one problem incessantly without growing weary.

reply by
THOMAS A. EDISON, when asked:
"What do you think is the first requisite
for success in your field, or any other?"

Concentration

You must be single minded. Drive for the one thing on which you have decided.

GEORGE S. PATTON

Gather in your resources, rally all your faculties, marshal all your energies, focus all your capacities upon mastery of at least one field of endeavor.

JOHN HAGGAI

The jack-of-all trades seldom is good at any. Concentrate all of your efforts on one definite chief aim.

NAPOLEON HILL

Concentrate; put all your eggs in one basket, and watch that basket....

ANDREW CARNEGIE

Success...it is focusing the full power of all you are on what you have a burning desire to achieve.

WILFERD A. PETERSON

We are aiming at consciously controlling our mental powers instead of letting them hurry us hither and thither in a purposeless manner....

THOMAS TROWARD

It is a process of diverting one's scattered forces into one powerful channel.

JAMES ALLEN

What a great discrepancy there is between men and the results they achieve! It is due to the difference in their power of calling together all the rays of their ability, and concentrating them upon one point.

ORISON SWETT MARDEN

Concentration, in its truest, unadulterated form, means being able to focus the mind on one single solitary thing.

KOMAR

Concentrate all your thoughts upon the work at hand. The sun's rays do not burn until brought to a focus.

ALEXANDER GRAHAM BELL

The weakest living creature, by concentrating his powers on a single object, can accomplish something; whereas the strongest, by dispersing his over many, may fail to accomplish anything.

THOMAS CARLYLE

What do I mean by concentration? I mean focusing totally on the business at hand and commanding your body to do exactly what you want it to do.

ARNOLD PALMER

Bring all your mind and faculties to bear without distraction on the problem or subject at hand....

WALTER G. OLEKSY

As the fletcher whittles and makes straight his arrows, so the master directs his straying thoughts.

GAUTAMA BUDDHA

When every physical and mental resource is focused, one's power to solve a problem multiplies tremendously.

NORMAN VINCENT PEALE

And herein lies the secret of true power. Learn, by constant practice, how to husband your resources, and concentrate them, at any moment, upon a given point.

JAMES ALLEN

Concentration

Nothing can add more power to your life than concentrating all of your energies on a limited set of targets.

NIDO QUBEIN

If you know how to bring all your forces together for battle, at the right moment, and in the right place, you don't need to have a large army to be successful....

MICHEL QUOIST

Persons with comparatively moderate powers will accomplish much, if they apply themselves wholly and indefatigably to one thing at a time.

SAMUEL SMILES

I always advise young men who write me on the subject to do one thing well, throwing all their energies into it.

JOHN WANAMAKER

Devote your entire will power to mastering one thing at a time; do not scatter your energies....

PARAMAHANSA YOGANANDA

Concentrate on one thing at a time, and rule out all outside influences that don't have any real bearing on the task at hand.

MARTY LIQUORI

The shortest way to do many things is to do only one thing at once.

RICHARD CECIL

To do two things at once is to do neither.

PUBLILIUS SYRUS

ou have to concentrate on one idea at a time.

ROBERT COLLIER

ou can do only one thing at a time....I simply tackle one problem and concentrate all efforts on what I am doing at the moment.

MAXWELL MALTZ

o one thing at a time extremely well, then move on to the next.

PETER NIVIO ZARLENGA

ery often we desire one thing and expect in our hearts another, which creates confusion. The master said, "A house divided against itself cannot stand."

RAYMOND HOLLIWELL

nd if a house be divided against itself, that house cannot stand.

Bible, MARK 3:25

nited we stand, divided we fall.

AESOP

ll power is feeble unless it is united.

JEAN DE LA FONTAINE

nion gives strength....

HOMER

ll your strength is in your union, All your danger is in discord.

HENRY WADSWORTH LONGFELLOW

Concentration

Your mind, which is yourself, can be likened to a house.... The first necessary move then, is to rid that house of all but the furnishings essential to success.

JOHN McDONALD

As every divided kingdom falls, so every mind divided between many studies confounds and saps itself.

LEONARDO DA VINCI

If you only care enough for a result, you will almost certainly attain it.... Only you must, then, really wish these things, and wish them exclusively, and not wish at the same time a hundred other incompatible things just as strongly.

WILLIAM JAMES

Above all be of single aim; have a legitimate and useful purpose, and devote yourself unreservedly to it.

JAMES ALLEN

Concentrate all your thoughts on the great desire in your life. This concentration must be continuous, unceasing—every minute; every hour; every day; every week.

CHARLES E. POPPLESTONE

Concentrate...for the greatest achievements are reserved for the man of single aim, in whom no rival powers divide the empire of the soul.

ORISON SWETT MARDEN

The secret to becoming confident is preparation. By practicing we come to a point of competence. We find ourselves accomplishing our goals gracefully and confidently. It is then that we do things

that we never dreamed we could do. We discover powers we never knew existed.

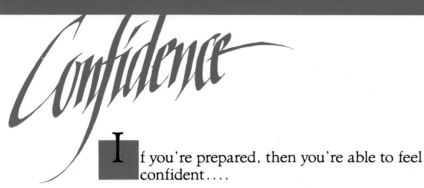

Confidence

If you're prepared, then you're able to feel confident....

ROBERT J. RINGER

There can be no great courage where there is no confidence or assurance, and half the battle is in the conviction that we can do what we undertake.

ORISON SWETT MARDEN

Confidence doesn't come out of nowhere. It's a result of something...hours and days and weeks and years of constant work and dedication.

ROGER STAUBACH

What I do is prepare myself until I know I can do what I have to do.

JOE NAMATH

For years I have been accused of making snap judgements. Honestly, this is not the case because I am a profound military student and the thoughts I express, perhaps too flippantly, are the result of years of thought and study.

GEORGE S. PATTON

It generally happens that assurance keeps an even pace with ability.

SAMUEL JOHNSON

e prepared!

BOY SCOUT MOTTO

Every conflict is a set of opposing ideas. All of us have had the feeling: knowing what we **should do** on the one hand, and doing what we **feel like doing** on the other. By

understanding these two opposing forces warring within us, we come to a knowledge of the truth: we no longer remain slaves. A clear understanding will make us masters.

Conflict

The most dramatic conflicts are perhaps, those that take place not between men but between a man and himself—where the arena of conflict is a solitary mind.

CLARK MOUSTAKAS

We have met the enemy...and they is us.

Pogo, WALT KELLY

Why don't you want to do what you know you should do? The reason you don't is that you're in conflict with yourself.

TOM HOPKINS

The split in you is clear....There is a part of you that knows what it should do, and a part that...does what it feels like doing.

JOHN CANTWELL KILEY

There are always two forces warring against each other within us.

PARAMAHANSA YOGANANDA

The spirit indeed is willing, but the flesh is weak.

Bible, MATTHEW 26:41

For the good that I would I do not: but the evil which I would not, that I do.

Bible, ROMANS 7:19

A man can do what he wants, but not want what he wants.

ARTHUR SCHOPENHAUER

What a man knows is everywhere at war with what he wants.

JOSEPH WOOD KRUTCH

We know better than we do. We do not yet possess ourselves....

RALPH WALDO EMERSON

A man's own self is his friend,
A man's own self is his foe.

BHAGAVAD-GITA

You are at enmity with yourself.

JACOB BOEHME

We are only falsehood, duplicity, contradiction; we both conceal and disguise ourselves from ourselves.

BLAISE PASCAL

This duality has been reflected in classical as well as modern literature as reason versus passion, or mind versus intuition....The split between the "conscious" mind and the "unconscious."....There are moments in each of our lives when our verbal-intellect suggests one course, and our "heart," or intuition, another.

ROBERT E. ORNSTEIN

Modern science knows much about such conflicts. We call the mental state that engenders it "ambivalence": a collision between thought and feeling.

DAVID SEABURY

The war existing between the senses and reason.

BLAISE PASCAL

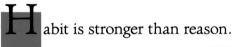

Conflict

Reason guides but a small part of man, and....The rest obeys feeling, true or false, and passion, good or bad.

JOSEPH ROUX

Habit is stronger than reason.

GEORGE SANTAYANA

The heart has its reasons which reason does not understand.

BLAISE PASCAL

Reason and emotion are not antagonists. What seems like a struggle is a struggle between two opposing ideas or values, one of which, automatic and unconscious, manifests itself in the form of a feeling.

NATHANIEL BRANDON

The subconscious part in us is called the subjective mind, because it does not decide and command. It is subject rather than a ruler. Its nature is to do what it is told, or what really in your heart of hearts you desire.

WILLIAM T. WALSH

One might as well try to ride two horses moving in different directions, as to try to maintain in equal force two opposing or contradictory sets of desires.

ROBERT COLLIER

If passion drives you, let reason hold the reins.

BENJAMIN FRANKLIN

In the end, we do battle only with ourselves. Once we understand this and focus our energy on what we can do to control our lives...we begin to gain important insights into how life works.

H. STANLEY JUDD

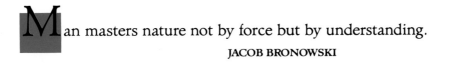

Man masters nature not by force but by understanding.

JACOB BRONOWSKI

We gain our ends only with the laws of nature; we control her only by understanding her laws.

JACOB BRONOWSKI

We cannot really think in one way and act in another....

THOMAS TROWARD

Feelings are nothing without the formulated idea that keeps them whole.

JACQUES BARZUN

When our knowing exceeds our sensing, we will no longer be deceived by the illusions of our senses.

WALTER RUSSELL

Without self-knowledge, without understanding the working and functions of his machine, man cannot be free, he cannot govern himself and he will always remain a slave....

GEORGE GURDJIEFF

It is part of our pedagogy to teach the operations of thinking, feeling, and willing so that they may be made conscious. For if we do not know the difference between an emotion and a thought, we will know very little ....We need to understand the components [of emotions] at work...in order to free their hold.

MARY CAROLINE RICHARDS

Our mission is to gain true discernment of the contraries, first as contraries, but then as poles of a unity.

HERMANN HESSE

Conflict

Become aware of internal, subjective, subverbal experiences, so that these experiences can be brought into the world of abstraction, of conversation, of naming, etc., with the consequence that it immediately becomes possible for a certain amount of control to be exerted over these hitherto unconscious and uncontrollable processes.

ABRAHAM H. MASLOW

A clear understanding of negative emotions dismisses them.

VERNON HOWARD

Talk back to your internal critic. Train yourself to recognize and write down critical thoughts as they go through your mind. Learn why these thoughts are untrue and practice talking and writing back to them.

ROBERT J. McKAIN

Something must be done when you find an opposing set of desires of this kind well to the fore in your category of strong desires. You must set in operation a process of competition, from which one must emerge a victor and the other set be defeated.

ROBERT COLLIER

Have a dialogue between the two opposing parts and you will find...that they always start out fighting each other,...until we come to an...appreciation of differences,...a oneness and integration of the two opposing forces. Then the civil war is finished, and your energies are ready for your struggle with the world.

FREDERICK PERLS

Insight into the two selves within a man clears up many confusions and contradictions....It was our understanding that preceded our victory.

VERNON HOWARD

We are enslaved by anything we do not consciously see. We are freed by conscious perception.

VERNON HOWARD

Instead of supressing conflicts, specific channels could be created to make this conflict explicit, and specific methods could be set up by which the conflict is resolved.

ALBERT LOW

We must become acquainted with our emotional household; we must see our feelings as they actually are, not as we assume they are. This breaks their hypnotic and damaging hold on us.

VERNON HOWARD

To be conscious that you are ignorant is a great step to knowledge.

BENJAMIN DISRAELI

We are slaves to whatever we don't understand.

VERNON HOWARD

And you will know the truth, and the truth will make you free.

Bible, JOHN 8:32

Resistance is thought transformed into feeling.... Change the thought that creates the resistance, and there is no more resistance.

BOB CONKLIN

The strong man is the one who is able to intercept at will the communication between the senses and the mind.

NAPOLEON BONAPARTE

Conflict

When we direct our thoughts properly, we can control our emotions....

W. CLEMENT STONE

When you do the wrong thing, knowing it is wrong, you do so because you haven't developed the habit of effectively controlling or neutralizing strong inner urges that tempt you, or because you have established the wrong habits and don't know how to eliminate them effectively.

W. CLEMENT STONE

It is only through your conscious mind that you can reach the subconscious.... Your conscious mind is the porter at the door, the watchman at the gate. It is to the conscious mind that the subconscious looks for all its impressions.

ROBERT COLLIER

He who would be useful, strong, and happy, must cease to be a passive receptacle for the negative, beggardly, and impure streams of thought; and as a wise householder commands his servants and invites his guests, so must he learn to command his desires, and to say, with authority, what thoughts he shall admit into the mansion of his soul.

JAMES ALLEN

Your answer to all this will be, "Obey. I am master here." Stand as master of your own being and hold your course steadfast to the goal.

JOHN McDONALD

When the fight begins within himself, a man's worth something.

ROBERT BROWNING

The major difference between people is that some succeed in mastering life, while others permit life to master them.

JAMES GORDON GILKEY

I have only one counsel for you—be master.

NAPOLEON BONAPARTE

Are we controlled by our thoughts, or are we controlling our thoughts?

RAYMOND HOLLIWELL

Your brain shall be your servant instead of your master. You will rule it instead of allowing it to rule you.

CHARLES E. POPPLESTONE

If you are ruled by mind you are a king; if by body, a slave.

CATO

If you do not conquer self, you will be conquered by self.

NAPOLEON HILL

Man who man would be, must rule the empire of himself.

PERCY BYSSHE SHELLEY

He who reins within himself and rules passions, desires, and fears is more than a king.

JOHN MILTON

I count him braver who overcomes his desires than him who conquers his enemies; for the hardest victory is the victory over self.

ARISTOTLE

The first and best victory is to conquer self.

PLATO

Conflict

There is no finer sensation in life than that which comes with victory over one's self....Go forward to a goal of inward achievement, brushing aside all your old internal enemies as you advance.

VASH YOUNG

It is better to conquer yourself than to win a thousand battles. Then the victory is yours. It cannot be taken from you, not by angels or by demons, heaven or hell.

GAUTAMA BUDDHA

He is great enough that is his own master.

JOSEPH HALL

Your real self—the "I am I"—is master of this land, the ruler of this empire...you rightfully have power and dominion over it, all its inhabitants, and all contained in its realm.

ROBERT COLLIER

The man who acquires the ability to take full possession of his own mind may take possession of anything else to which he is justly entitled.

ANDREW CARNEGIE

Give me beauty in the inward soul; may the outward and the inward man be at one.

SOCRATES

We are in control to the degree that we make the decisions. To affect the outcome of anything, we must control the action at the point of decision making. If we let others make decisions for

us, we have no control. When we control the decisions, we control the actions.

Control

To decide, to be at the level of choice, is to take responsibility for your life and to be in control of your life.

ARBIE M. DALE

When you take charge of your life, there is no longer need to ask permission of other people or society at large....When you ask permission, you give someone veto power over your life.

GEOFFRY F. ABERT

If you don't run your own life, somebody else will.

JOHN ATKINSON

Sometimes if you want to see a change for the better, you have to take things into your own hands.

CLINT EASTWOOD

If you want a thing done well, do it yourself.

NAPOLEON BONAPARTE

The greatest potential for control tends to exist at the point where action takes place.

LOUIS A. ALLEN

The question is...who's to be master?

LEWIS CARROLL, (paraphrased)
Through the Looking-Glass

If not you, then who?
If not now, then when?

HILLEL

We gain what we want through

the help and support of others.

Cooperation

To be agreeable, to be liked, to

cooperate—this contributes

immeasurably to our success.

When we coordinate our efforts

with the efforts of others, we

speed the way to our goals.

Cooperation builds success.

Cooperation

The world basically and fundamentally is constituted on the basis of harmony. Everything works in co-operation with something else.

PRESTON BRADLEY

No employer today is independent of those about him. He cannot succeed alone, no matter how great his ability or capital. Business today is more than ever a question of cooperation.

ORISON SWETT MARDEN

Personal relationships are the fertile soil from which all advancement, all success, all achievement in real life grows.

BEN STEIN

It is...through cooperation, rather than conflict, that your greatest successes will be derived....

RALPH CHARELL

There is no such thing as a self-made man. You will reach your goals only with the help of others.

GEORGE SHINN

Here is a basic rule for winning success. Let's mark it in the mind and remember it. The rule is: Success depends on the support of other people. The only hurdle between you and what you want to be is the support of others.

DAVID JOSEPH SCHWARTZ

No young man starting in life could have better capital than plenty of friends. They will strengthen his credit, support him in every great effort, and make him what, unaided, he could never be. Friends of the right sort will help him more—to be happy and successful—than much money....

ORISON SWETT MARDEN

I would rather have a million friends than a million dollars.

EDWARD VERNON RICKENBACKER

W in hearts, and you have hands and purses.

LORD BURLEIGH

N ow you can begin to see quite transparently that the entire game of life is one of agreement. If other people don't agree with you you're in big trouble. How far would you get in your work if nobody agreed that what you were doing had value?

CARL FREDERICK

A lways think in terms of what the other person wants.

JAMES VAN FLEET

I believe that you can get everything in life you want if you will just help enough other people get what they want.

ZIG ZIGLAR

I f your imagination leads you to understand how quickly people grant your requests when those requests appeal to their self-interest, you can have practically anything you go after.

NAPOLEON HILL

T here is nothing wrong in using people. The success never uses people except to their advantage.

MARK CAINE

S uccess depends on our using, and not opposing....

THOMAS TROWARD

Cooperation

The duty of helping one's self in the highest sense involves the helping of one's neighbours.

SAMUEL SMILES

It is literally true that you can succeed best and quickest by helping others to succeed.

NAPOLEON HILL

Always try to do something for the other fellow and you will be agreeably surprised how things come your way—how many pleasant things are done for you.

CLAUDE M. BRISTOL

Doing things for others always pays dividends....

CLAUDE M. BRISTOL

He that does good to another does good also to himself....

SENECA

He who wished to secure the good of others, has already secured his own.

CONFUCIUS

Help thy brother's boat across, and lo! thine own has reached the shore.

HINDU PROVERB

We cannot hold a torch to light another's path without brightening our own.

BEN SWEETLAND

It is one of the beautiful compensations of this life that no one can sincerely try to help another without helping himself.

CHARLES DUDLEY WARNER

You are beginning to see that any man to whom you can do a favor is your friend, and that you can do a favor to almost anyone.

MARK CAINE

There is nothing that puts a man more in your debt than that he owes you nothing.

MARK CAINE

Put yourself in the other man's place, and then you will know why he thinks certain things and does certain deeds.

ELBERT HUBBARD

Take the trouble to stop and think of the other person's feelings, his viewpoints, his desires and needs. Think more of what the other fellow wants, and how he must feel.

MAXWELL MALTZ

We cannot live only for ourselves. A thousand fibers connect us with our fellow-men....

HERMAN MELVILLE

No man is an island, entire of itself; every man is a piece of the continent, a part of the main.

JOHN DONNE

How strange is the lot of us mortals! Each of us is here for a brief sojourn; for what purpose he knows not, though he senses it. But without deeper reflection one knows from daily life that one exists for other people.

ALBERT EINSTEIN

Cooperation

No man has come to true greatness who has not felt that his life belongs to his race, and that which God gives to him, He gives him for mankind.

PHILLIPS BROOKS

What do we live for; if it is not to make life less difficult to each other?

GEORGE ELIOT

I think we're here for each other.

CAROL BURNETT

We do not exist for ourselves....

THOMAS MERTON

Men exist for the sake of one another.

MARCUS AURELIUS

Coming together is a beginning;
Keeping together is progress;
Working together is success.

HENRY FORD

Courage is the power to face difficulties. It's the opposite of being **dis**couraged. Courage comes from a reserve of mind more powerful than outside circumstances. When

we are bigger than our problems, we gain the courage necessary to win.

Courage

Courage consists in equality to the problem before us.

RALPH WALDO EMERSON

Be larger than your task.

ORISON SWETT MARDEN

Do not pray for tasks equal to your powers. Pray for powers equal to your tasks.

PHILLIPS BROOKS

The pressure of adversity does not affect the mind of the brave man.... It is more powerful than external circumstances.

SENECA

Nothing splendid has ever been achieved except by those who dared believe that something inside of them was superior to circumstance.

BRUCE BARTON

Man is not the creature of circumstances, circumstances are the creatures of men. We are free agents, and man is more powerful than matter.

BENJAMIN DISRAELI

He that would be superior to external influences must first become superior to his own passions.

SAMUEL JOHNSON

Allow motion to equal emotion.

ELBERT HUBBARD

Obstacles will look large or small to you according to whether you are large or small.

ORISON SWETT MARDEN

What the superior man seeks is in himself: what the small man seeks is in others.

FRANCOIS LA ROCHEFOUCAULD

You are merely not feeling equal to the tasks before you.

DALE CARNEGIE

The obstacles you face are...mental barriers which can be broken by adopting a more positive approach.

CLARENCE BLASIER

Quit thinking that you must halt before the barrier of inner negativity. You need not. You can crash through ....Wherever we see a negative state, that is where we can destroy it.

VERNON HOWARD

A barrier is of ideas, not of things.

MARK CAINE

Stone walls do not a prison make, nor iron bars a cage.

RICHARD LOVELACE

We are the prisoners of ideas.

RALPH WALDO EMERSON

Make not your thoughts your prisons.

WILLIAM SHAKESPEARE

All of the significant battles are waged within the self.

SHELDON KOPP

Courage

This is where you will win the battle—in the playhouse of your mind.

MAXWELL MALTZ

Courage is the capacity to confront what can be imagined....

LEO ROSTEN

True courage is a result of reasoning. A brave mind is always impregnable.

JEREMY COLLIER

Courage is resistance to fear, mastery of fear—not absence of fear.

MARK TWAIN

Victory becomes, to some degree, a state of mind. Knowing ourselves superior to the anxieties, troubles, and worries which obsess us, we are superior to them.

BASIL KING

Courage is a special kind of knowledge: the knowledge of how to fear what ought to be feared and how not to fear what ought not to be feared.

DAVID BEN-GURION

Much of what we call evil is due entirely to the way men take the phenomenon. It can so often be converted into a bracing and tonic good by a simple change of the sufferer's inner attitude from one of fear to one of fight; its sting can so often depart and turn into a relish when, after vainly seeking to shun it, we agree to face about and bear it....

WILLIAM JAMES

The beauty of the soul shines out when a man bears with composure one heavy mischance after another, not because he does not feel them, but because he is a man of high and heroic temper.

ARISTOTLE

This is the test of your manhood: How much is there left in you after you have lost everything outside of yourself?

ORISON SWETT MARDEN

What you have outside you counts less than what you have inside you.

B. C. FORBES

If I were asked to give what I consider the single most useful bit of advice for all humanity it would be this: Expect trouble as an inevitable part of life and when it comes, hold your head high, look it squarely in the eye and say, "I will be bigger than you. You cannot defeat me."

ANN LANDERS

To have character is to be big enough to take life on.

MARY CAROLINE RICHARDS

It is not the situation that makes the man, but the man who makes the situation.

FREDERICK W. ROBERTSON

Let us train our minds to desire what the situation demands.

SENECA

Nothing external to you has any power over you.

RALPH WALDO EMERSON

Courage

Little minds attain and are subdued by misfortunes; but great minds rise above them.

WASHINGTON IRVING

**R**eality is something you rise above.

LIZA MINNELLI

I am bigger than anything that can happen to me.

CHARLES F. LUMMIS

I am more important than my problems.

JOSE FERRER

We are no longer puppets being manipulated by outside powerful forces; we become the powerful force ourselves.

LEO BUSCAGLIA

Progress begins a step at a time. There is no sudden leap to greatness. Our success lies in doing day by day. The upward reach comes from

Cumulative Results

working carefully and well. Good work done little by little becomes a great work. The house of success is built brick by brick.

Cumulative Results

Successful action is cumulative in its results.

WALLACE D. WATTLES

No great thing is created suddenly, any more than a bunch of grapes or a fig. If you tell me that you desire a fig, I answer you that there must be time. Let it first blossom, then bear fruit, then ripen.

EPICTETUS

Progress, however, of the best kind, is comparatively slow. Great results cannot be achieved at once; and we must be satisfied to advance in life as we walk, step by step.

SAMUEL SMILES

The most successful men in the end are those whose success is the result of steady accretion.... It is the man who carefully advances step by step, with his mind becoming wider and wider,—and progressively better able to grasp any theme or situation,—persevering in what he knows to be practical, and concentrating his thought upon it, who is bound to succeed in the greatest degree.

ALEXANDER GRAHAM BELL

There is no sudden leap into the stratosphere.... There is only advancing step by step, slowly and tortuously, up the pyramid toward your goals....

BEN STEIN

Success is the sum of small efforts, repeated day in and day out....

ROBERT COLLIER

My success just evolved from working hard at the business at hand each day.

JOHNNY CARSON

If we triumph in the little things of our common hours, we are sure to triumph in our lives.

UNKNOWN

Life is a series of steps. Things are done gradually. Once in a while there is a giant step, but most of the time we are taking small, seemingly insignificant steps on the stairway of life.

RALPH RANSOM

The person determined to achieve maximum success learns the principle that progress is made one step at a time. A house is built a brick at a time. Football games are won a play at a time. A department store grows bigger one customer at a time. Every big accomplishment is a series of little accomplishments.

DAVID JOSEPH SCHWARTZ

I have tried to make all my acts and commercial moves the result of definite consideration and sound judgement. There were never any great ventures or risks. I practiced honest, slow-growing business methods, and tried to back them with energy and good system.

MARSHALL FIELD

Every action is either strong or weak, and when every action is strong we are successful.

WALLACE D. WATTLES

Success is the sum of detail.

HARVEY S. FIRESTONE

All great masters are chiefly distinguished by the power of adding a second, a third, and perhaps a fourth step in a continuous line. Many a man had taken the first step. With every additional step you enhance immensely the value of your first.

RALPH WALDO EMERSON

Cumulative Results

You can do what you want to do, accomplish what you want to accomplish, attain any reasonable objective you may have in mind—not all of a sudden, perhaps not in one swift and sweeping act of achievement— but you can do it gradually, day by day and play by play, if you want to do it, if you work to do it, over a sufficiently long period of time.

WILLIAM E. HOLLER

There is no royal road to anything. One thing at a time, all things in succession. That which grows fast, withers as rapidly. That which grows slowly, endures.

JOSIAH GILBERT HOLLAND

Let me look upward into the branches of the flowering oak and know that it grew great and strong because it grew slowly and well.

WILFERD A. PETERSON

Adopt the pace of nature: her secret is patience.

RALPH WALDO EMERSON

Perfection is attained by slow degrees; she requires the hand of time.

VOLTAIRE

Well being is attained by little and little, and nevertheless it is no little thing itself.

ZENO OF CITIUM

Nothing can be done except little by little.

CHARLES BAUDELAIRE

Little by little does the trick.

AESOP

ne may walk over the highest mountain one step at a time.

JOHN WANAMAKER

ll difficult things have their origin in that which is easy, and great things in that which is small.

LAO-TZU

he fall of dropping water wears away the stone.

LUCRETIUS

 jug fills drop by drop.

GAUTAMA BUDDHA

any strokes overthrow the tallest oaks.

JOHN LYLY

verything in life is a progression of steps.

SCOTT REED

f you should put even a little on a little and should do this often, soon this would become big.

HESIOD

 little and little, collected together, become a great deal; the heap in the barn consists of single grains, and drop and drop make the inundation.

SA'DI

o not despise the bottom rungs in the ascent to greatness.

PUBLILIUS SYRUS

Cumulative Results

The loftiest edifices need the deepest foundations.

GEORGE SANTAYANA

You can't start at the top.

SAMUEL LEVENSON

Instead of rising rapidly in the beginning and flattening out later, the earnings curves of most of those who eventually became millionaires was the reverse: their income increased slowly, if at all, for many years. And then, after two to three decades, it suddenly went through the roof.

SRULLY BLOTNICK

Let this be understood, then, at starting; that the patient conquest of difficulties which rise in the regular and legitimate channels of business and enterprise is not only essential in securing the success which you seek but it is essential to that preparation of your mind, requisite for the enjoyment of your successes, and for retaining them when gained.... So, day by day, and week by week; so, month after month, and year after year, work on, and in that process gain strength and symmetry, and nerve and knowledge, that when success, patiently and bravely worked for, shall come, it may find you prepared to receive it and keep it.

JOSIAH GILBERT HOLLAND

Build today, then, strong and sure,
With a firm and ample base;
And ascending and secure
Shall tomorrow find its place.

HENRY WADSWORTH LONGFELLOW

There is no road too long to the man who advances deliberately and without undue haste; there are no honors too distant to the man who prepares himself for them with patience.

JEAN DE LA BRUYÈRE

Events tend to repeat themselves. The tide of opportunity comes to us all.

And when we are prepared for opportunity, our chance is sure to come. Success doesn't depend upon being at the right place at the right time—it depends upon being ready.

Cycles

Events tend to recur in cycles....

W. CLEMENT STONE

Each thing is of like form from everlasting and comes round again in its cycle....

MARCUS AURELIUS

By the law of periodical repetition, everything which has happened once must happen again and again and again—and not capriciously, but at regular periods, and each thing in its own period, not another's, and each obeying its own law....

MARK TWAIN

What has been will be again, what has been done will be done again....

Bible, ECCLESIASTES 1:9

Whatever is has already been, and what will be has been before....

Bible, ECCLESIASTES 3:15

That which the fountain sends forth returns again to the fountain.

HENRY WADSWORTH LONGFELLOW

All motion is cyclic. It circulates to the limits of its possibilities and then returns to its starting point.

ROBERT COLLIER

All patterned forms repeat their pattern sequentially.

J. G. GALLIMORE

Was it not a comedy, a strange and stupid thing, this repetition, this course of events in a fateful circle?....Everything that was not suffered to the end and finally concluded, recurred....

HERMANN HESSE

Why abandon a belief merely because it ceases to be true? Cling to it long enough and...it will turn true again, for so it goes. Most of the change we think we see in life is due to truths being in and out of favor.

ROBERT FROST

There is a tide in the affairs of men, which, taken at the flood, leads on to fortune....

WILLIAM SHAKESPEARE

I think luck is the sense to recognize an opportunity and the ability to take advantage of it....The man who can smile at his breaks and grab his chances gets on.

SAMUEL GOLDWYN

Be ready when opportunity comes....Luck is the time when preparation and opportunity meet.

ROY D. CHAPIN, JR.

Experience has taught me this, that we undo ourselves by impatience. Misfortunes have their life and their limits, their sickness and their health.

MICHEL EYQUEM DE MONTAIGNE

The only sure thing about luck is that it will change.

WILSON MIZNER, also attributed to
BRET HARTE

Give wind and tide a chance to change.

RICHARD E. BYRD

Cycles

Everything comes if a man will only wait.

BENJAMIN DISRAELI

The philosophy of waiting is sustained by all the oracles of the universe.

RALPH WALDO EMERSON

Wealth is in applications of mind to nature; and the art of getting rich consists not in industry, much less in saving, but in a better order, in timeliness, in being at the right spot.

RALPH WALDO EMERSON

Luck is being at the right place at the right time, but location and timing are to some extent under our control.

NATASHA JOSEFOWITZ

It is a great piece of skill to know how to guide your luck even while waiting for it.

BALTASAR GRACIÁN

This is the law of prosperity. When apparent adversity comes, be not cast down by it, but make the best of it, and always look forward for better things, for conditions more prosperous.

RALPH WALDO TRINE

All of us have bad luck and good luck. The man who persists through the bad luck—who keeps right on going—is the man who is there when the good luck comes—and is ready to receive it.

ROBERT COLLIER

The season of failure is the best time for sowing the seeds of success.

PARAMAHANSA YOGANANDA

Too often man handles life as he does the bad weather. He whiles away the time as he waits for it to stop.

ALFRED POLGAR

For all your days prepare,
And meet them ever alike:
When you are the anvil, bear;
When you are the hammer, strike.

EDWIN MARKHAM

When ye are prepared for a thing, the opportunity to use it presents itself.

EDGAR CAYCE

Chance favors the prepared mind.

LOUIS PASTEUR

I will prepare and some day my chance will come.

ABRAHAM LINCOLN

Unless you have prepared yourself to profit by your chance, the opportunity will only make you ridiculous. A great occasion is valuable to you just in proportion as you have educated yourself to make use of it.

ORISON SWETT MARDEN

Talent alone won't make you a success. Neither will being in the right place at the right time, unless you are ready. The most important question is: "Are you ready?"

JOHNNY CARSON

The secret of success in life is for a man to be ready for his opportunity when it comes.

BENJAMIN DISRAELI

Cycles

Luck can often mean simply taking advantage of a situation at the right moment. It is possible to "make" your luck by being always prepared.

MICHAEL KORDA

Some say opportunity knocks only once. That is not true. Opportunity knocks all the time, but you have to be ready for it. If the chance comes, you must have the equipment to take advantage of it.

LOUIS L'AMOUR

A good deal happens in a man's life that he isn't responsible for. Fortunate openings occur; but it is safe to remember that such "breaks" are occurring all the time, and other things being equal, the advantage goes to the man who is ready.

LAWRENCE DOWNS

Take a second look at what appears to be someone's "good luck." You'll find not luck but preparation, planning, and success-producing thinking....

DAVID JOSEPH SCHWARTZ

Luck means...the long nights you have devoted to work....The trains you have never failed to catch.

MAX O'RELL

The race is not to the swift or the battle to the strong...but time and chance happen to them all.

Bible, ECCLESIASTES 9:11

wise man turns chance into good fortune.

THOMAS FULLER

There is a key which, if
properly used and understood,
will ensure the success of any
endeavor—the key is desire. If
we are willing to pay any
price—even our circumstances
change. If we want something

badly enough, we are sure to
get it. If we have the desire,
we have the power.

Desire

A will finds a way.

ORISON SWETT MARDEN

"**W**here there is a will there is a way," is an old and true saying. He who resolves upon doing a thing, by that very resolution often scales the barriers to it, and secures its achievement. To think we are able, is almost to be so—to determine upon attainment is frequently attainment itself.

SAMUEL SMILES

Desire creates the power.

RAYMOND HOLLIWELL

Where there is no power...there is never any desire to do a thing; and where there is strong desire to do a thing...the power to do it is strong.

WALLACE D. WATTLES

There is nothing capricious in nature and the implanting of a desire indicates that its gratification is in the constitution of the creature that feels it.

RALPH WALDO EMERSON

Desire is proof of the availability....

ROBERT COLLIER

You are never given a wish without also being given the power to make it true.

RICHARD BACH

There are ways which lead to everything, and if we have sufficient will we should always have sufficient means.

FRANCOIS LA ROCHEFOUCAULD

You learn that, whatever you are doing in life, obstacles don't matter very much. Pain or other circumstances can be there, but if you want to do a job bad enough, you'll find a way to get it done.

JACK YOUNGBLOOD

One essential to success is that your desire be an all-obsessing one, your thoughts and aims be co-ordinated, and your energy be concentrated and applied without letup.

CLAUDE M. BRISTOL

Very few persons, comparatively, know how to Desire with sufficient intensity. . . . They do not know what it is to feel and manifest that intense, eager, longing, craving, insistent, demanding, ravenous Desire which is akin to the persistent, insistent, ardent, overwhelming desire of the drowning man for a breath of air; of the shipwrecked or desert-lost man for a drink of water; of the famished man for bread and meat. . . .

ROBERT COLLIER

This force, which is the best thing in you, your highest self, will never respond to any ordinary half-hearted call, or any milk-and-water endeavor. It can only be reached by your supremest call, your supremest effort. It will respond only to the call that is backed up by the whole of you, not part of you; you must be all there in what you are trying to do. You must bring every particle of your energy, unswervable resolution, your best efforts, your persistent industry to your task or the best will not come out of you. You must back up your ambition by your whole nature, by unbounded enthusiasm and a determination to win which knows no failure. . . . Only a masterly call, a masterly will, a supreme effort, intense and persistent application, can unlock the door to your inner treasure and release your highest powers.

ORISON SWETT MARDEN

Desire

The greatest trouble with most of us is that our demands upon ourselves are so feeble, the call upon the great within of us so weak and intermittent that it makes no impression upon the creative energies; it lacks the force that transmutes desires into realities.

ORISON SWETT MARDEN

Only one thing...a desire so strong, a determination so intense, that you cheerfully throw everything you have into the scale to win what you want. Not merely your work and your money and your thought, but the willingness to stand or fall by the result—to do or to die.

ROBERT COLLIER

It is only when you despair of all ordinary means, it is only when you convince it that it must help you or you perish, that the seed of life in you bestirs itself to provide a new resource.

ROBERT COLLIER

You know from past experiences that whenever you have been driven to the wall, or thought you were, you have extricated yourself in a way which you never would have dreamed possible had you not been put to the test. The trouble is that in your everyday life you don't go deep enough to tap the divine mind within you.

ORISON SWETT MARDEN

Mind is all that counts. You can be whatever you make up your mind to be.

ROBERT COLLIER

I have always believed that anybody with a little guts and the desire to apply himself can make it, can make anything he wants to make of himself.

WILLIE SHOEMAKER

ou can really have everything you want, if you go after it. But you will have to want it. The desire for success must be so strong within you that it is the very breath of your life—your first thought when you awaken in the morning, your last thought when you go to bed at night....

CHARLES E. POPPLESTONE

A man can do anything he wants to do in this world, at least if he wants to do it badly enough.

E. W. SCRIPPS

ou can have anything you want—if you want it badly enough. You can be anything you want to be, have anything you desire, accomplish anything you set out to accomplish—if you will hold to that desire with singleness of purpose....

ROBERT COLLIER

he thing that contributes to anyone's reaching the goal he wants is simply wanting that goal badly enough.

CHARLES E. WILSON

Anything you really want, you can attain, if you really go after it.

WAYNE DYER

The longer I live, the more I am certain that the great difference between men, between the feeble and the powerful, between the great and the insignificant, is energy—invincible determination—a purpose once fixed, and then death or victory.

SIR THOMAS FOWELL BUXTON

I have brought myself, by long meditation, to the conviction that a human being with a settled purpose must accomplish it, and that nothing can resist a will which will stake even existence upon its fulfillment.

BENJAMIN DISRAELI

Desire

All our dreams can come true—if we have the courage to pursue them.

WALT DISNEY

Dreams do come true, if we only wish hard enough. You can have anything in life if you will sacrifice everything else for it.

SIR JAMES M. BARRIE

If we enjoy what we do, we will be successful. If we do not enjoy what we do, we will not

Enjoyment

be successful. Our success in any occupation depends upon enjoyment. Loving our work makes the difference. He who finds joy in his work, has found success at last.

Enjoyment

You never achieve real success unless you like what you are doing.

DALE CARNEGIE

No man can succeed in a line of endeavor which he does not like.

NAPOLEON HILL

No man is a success in business unless he loves his work.

FLORENCE SCOVEL SHINN

If you cannot work with love but only with distaste, it is better that you should leave your work....

KAHLIL GIBRAN

If you don't love something, then don't do it.

RAY BRADBURY

If you don't get a kick out of the job you're doing you'd better hunt another one.

SAMUEL VAUCLAIN

Like what you do, if you don't like it, do something else.

PAUL HARVEY

Your chances of success are directly proportional to the degree of pleasure you derive from what you do. If you are in a job you hate, face the fact squarely and get out.

MICHAEL KORDA

I'd rather be a failure in something that I love than a success in something that I don't.

GEORGE BURNS

You will never succeed while smarting under the drudgery of your occupation, if you are constantly haunted with the idea that you could succeed better in something else.

ORISON SWETT MARDEN

What you do is more important than how much you make, and how you feel about it is more important than what you do.

JERRY GILLIES

The more you love what you are doing, the more successful it will be for you.

JERRY GILLIES

If you do not feel yourself growing in your work and your life broadening and deepening, if your task is not a perpetual tonic to you, you have not found your place.

ORISON SWETT MARDEN

The first essential in a boy's career is to find out what he's fitted for, what he's most capable of doing and doing with a relish.

CHARLES M. SCHWAB

It is what we do easily and what we like to do that we do well.

ORISON SWETT MARDEN

Everyone enjoys doing the kind of work for which he is best suited.

NAPOLEON HILL

Enjoyment

No man can be ideally successful until he has found his place. Like a locomotive he is strong on the track, but weak anywhere else.

ORISON SWETT MARDEN

Whatever you are by nature, keep to it; never desert your line of talent. Be what nature intended you for, and you will succeed....

SYDNEY SMITH

You've got to like your work. You've got to like what you are doing, you've got to be doing something worthwhile so you can like it—because if it's worthwhile, that makes a difference, don't you see?

COLONEL HARLAND SANDERS

Get into a line that you will find to be a deep personal interest, something you really enjoy spending twelve to fifteen hours a day working at, and the rest of the time thinking about.

EARL NIGHTINGALE

You have not found your place until all your faculties are roused, and your whole nature consents and approves of the work you are doing....

ORISON SWETT MARDEN

A man must get his happiness out of his work.... Without work he enjoys, he can never know what happiness is.

THOMAS CARLYLE

Far and away the best prize that life offers is the chance to work hard at work worth doing.

THEODORE ROOSEVELT

There is nothing better for a man, than that he should eat and drink, and that he should make his soul enjoy good in his labour.

Bible, ECCLESIASTES 2:24

The crowning fortune of a man is to be born to some pursuit which finds him in employment and happiness, whether it be to make baskets, or broadswords, or canals, or statues, or songs.

RALPH WALDO EMERSON

Success in its highest and noblest form calls for peace of mind and enjoyment and happiness which come only to the man who has found the work that he likes best.

NAPOLEON HILL

Blessed is the man who has some congenial work, some occupation in which he can put his heart, and which affords a complete outlet to all the forces there are in him.

JOHN BURROUGHS

There is some place where your specialness can shine. Somewhere that difference can be expressed. It's up to you to find it, and you can.

DAVID VISCOTT

The man who does not work for the love of work but only for money is not likely to make money nor to find much fun in life.

CHARLES M. SCHWAB

Don't set compensation as a goal. Find work you like, and the compensation will follow.

HARDING LAWRENCE

Enjoyment

The fact remains that the overwhelming majority of people who have become wealthy have become so thanks to work they found profoundly absorbing. . . . The long-term study of people who eventually became wealthy clearly reveals that their "luck" arose from the accidental dedication they had to an area they enjoyed.

SRULLY BLOTNICK

I never did a day's work in my life. It was all fun.

THOMAS A. EDISON

You don't pay the price for success. You enjoy the price for success.

ZIG ZIGLAR

Our work and our play. All our pleasures experienced as the pleasure of love. What could be better than that? To feel in one's work the tender and flushed substance of one's dearest concern.

MARY CAROLINE RICHARDS

Do what you love. Know your own bone; gnaw at it, bury it, unearth it, and gnaw it still.

HENRY DAVID THOREAU

Work is not man's punishment. It is his reward and his strength and his pleasure.

GEORGE SAND

Work is love made visible.

KAHLIL GIBRAN

We become like our

environment, and our

environment becomes like

us. Everything around

us molds and shapes us.

So it is important to

choose our environment

with care: one that is

positive, one that lifts

us up and gives us

wings to soar.

Environment

We shape our buildings; thereafter they shape us.

WINSTON CHURCHILL

Man shapes himself through decisions that shape his environment.

RENÉ DUBOS

When we become a part of anything, it becomes a part of us.

DAVID HAROLD FINK

I am part of all that I have met....

ALFRED LORD TENNYSON

Every experience in life, everything with which we have come in contact in life, is a chisel which has been cutting away at our life statue, molding, modifying, shaping it. We are part of all we have met. Everything we have seen, heard, felt or thought has had its hand in molding us, shaping us.

ORISON SWETT MARDEN

You are a product of your environment. So choose the environment that will best develop you toward your objective. Analyze your life in terms of its environment. Are the things around you helping you toward success—or are they holding you back?

W. CLEMENT STONE

Your outlook upon life, your estimate of yourself, your estimate of your value are largely colored by your environment. Your whole career will be modified, shaped, molded by your surroundings, by the character of the people with whom you come in contact every day....

ORISON SWETT MARDEN

We are shaped by each other. We adjust not to the reality of a world but to the reality of other thinkers.

JOSEPH CHILTON PEARCE

Every man is like the company he is wont to keep.

EURIPIDES

Wherever you are it is your own friends who make your world.

RALPH BARTON PERRY

Keep away from people who try to belittle your ambition. Small people always do that, but the really great make you feel that you, too, can become great.

MARK TWAIN

We begin to see, therefore, the importance of selecting our environment with the greatest of care, because environment is the mental feeding ground out of which the food that goes into our minds is extracted.

NAPOLEON HILL

The first step toward success is taken when you refuse to be a captive of the environment in which you first find yourself.

MARK CAINE

The first step toward getting somewhere is to decide that you are not going to stay where you are.

JOHN J. B. MORGAN and
EWING T. WEBB

The reasonable man adapts himself to the world; the unreasonable one persists in trying to adapt the world to himself. Therefore all progress depends on the unreasonable man.

GEORGE BERNARD SHAW

Environment

A strong, successful man is not the victim of his environment. He creates favorable conditions. His own inherent force and energy compel things to turn out as he desires.

ORISON SWETT MARDEN

We make the world we live in and shape our own environment.

ORISON SWETT MARDEN

Your world is a living expression of how you are using and have used your mind.

EARL NIGHTINGALE

We live in a web of ideas, a fabric of our own making.

JOSEPH CHILTON PEARCE

People blame their environment.... There is one person to blame—and only one—themselves.

ROBERT COLLIER

We are the environment.

CHARLES PANATI

You can never really get away—you can only take yourself somewhere else.

SCHWAB'S COMMENTARY

Home is where the heart is.

PLINY THE ELDER

I ask my mind: What is your habitat? What or where or when do you feel at home?

R. D. LAING

Going far beyond the call of
duty, doing more than others
expect—this is what excellence
is all about. And it comes from

striving, maintaining the
highest standards, looking after
the smallest detail, and going
the extra mile. Excellence
means caring—it means making
a special effort to do more.

Excellence

Always do more than is required of you.

GEORGE S. PATTON

Do a little more each day than you think you possibly can.

LOWELL THOMAS

All successful employers are stalking men who will do the unusual, men who think, men who attract attention by performing more than is expected of them.

CHARLES M. SCHWAB

The kind of people I look for to fill top management spots are the eager beavers, the mavericks. These are the guys who try to do more than they're expected to do—they always reach.

LEE IACOCCA

Excellence means when a man or woman asks of himself more than others do.

ORTEGA Y GASSET

People who have accomplished work worth while have had a very high sense of the way to do things. They have not been content with mediocrity. They have not confined themselves to the beaten tracks; they have never been satisfied to do things just as others do them, but always a little better. They always pushed things that came to their hands a little higher up, a little farther on. It is this little higher up, this little farther on, that counts in the quality of life's work. It is the constant effort to be first-class in everything one attempts that conquers the heights of excellence.

ORISON SWETT MARDEN

To do the right thing, at the right time, in the right way; to do some things better than they were ever done before; to eliminate errors; to know both sides of the question; to be courteous; to be an example; to work for the love of work; to anticipate requirements; to develop resources; to recognize no impediments; to master circumstances; to act from reason rather than rule; to be satisfied with nothing short of perfection.

MARSHALL FIELD & COMPANY

Great men are little men expanded; great lives are ordinary lives intensified.

WILFERD A. PETERSON

Great men are but common men more fully developed and ripened.

ORISON SWETT MARDEN

The uncommon man is merely the common man thinking and dreaming of success in larger terms and in more fruitful areas.

MELVIN POWERS

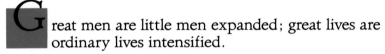Doing the common things uncommonly well....

ORISON SWETT MARDEN

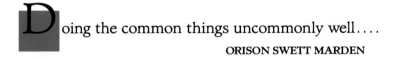Doing ordinary things extraordinarily well.

JOHN W. GARDNER

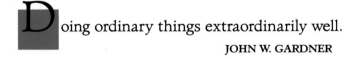Put the uncommon effort into the common task... make it large by doing it in a great way.

ORISON SWETT MARDEN

It is not the straining for great things that is most effective; it is the doing the little things, the common duties, a little better and better....

ORISON SWETT MARDEN

Excellence

True greatness consists in being great in little things.

CHARLES SIMMONS

I can do small things in a great way.

JAMES FREEMAN CLARKE

It is quality rather than quantity that matters.

SENECA

He who has put a good finish to his undertaking is said to have placed a golden crown to the whole.

EUSTACHIUS

Trifles make perfection, and perfection is no trifle.

MICHELANGELO

The only certain means of success is to render more and better service than is expected of you, no matter what your task may be.

OG MANDINO

Here is the simple but powerful rule...always give people more than they expect to get.

NELSON BOSWELL

You can start right where you stand and apply the habit of going the extra mile by rendering more service and better service than you are now being paid for....

NAPOLEON HILL

And whosoever shall compel thee to go a mile, go with him twain.

Bible, MATTHEW 5:41

The success combination in business is: Do what you do better...and: Do more of what you do....

DAVID JOSEPH SCHWARTZ

To enjoy enduring success we should travel a little in advance of the world.

JOHN McDONALD

I start where the last man left off.

THOMAS A. EDISON

The man who comes up with a means for doing or producing almost anything better, faster or more economically has his future and his fortune at his fingertips.

J. PAUL GETTY

There is always a best way of doing everything....

RALPH WALDO EMERSON

There's a way to do it better...find it.

THOMAS A. EDISON

There is an infinite difference between a little wrong and just right, between fairly good and the best, between mediocrity and superiority....

ORISON SWETT MARDEN

Make it a life-rule to give your best to whatever passes through your hands. Stamp it with your manhood. Let superiority be your trademark....

ORISON SWETT MARDEN

Superiority—doing things a little better than anybody else can do them.

ORISON SWETT MARDEN

Excellence

It is just the little difference between the good and the best that makes the difference between the artist and the artisan. It is just the little touches after the average man would quit that make the master's fame.

ORISON SWETT MARDEN

Much good work is lost for the lack of a little more.

E. H. HARRIMAN

Do a little bit more than average and from that point on our progress multiplies itself out of all proportion to the effort put in.

PAUL J. MEYER

Do more than you're supposed to do and you can have or be or do anything you want.

BILL SANDS

Do your work; not just your work and no more, but a little more for the lavishings sake—that little more which is worth all the rest.

DEAN BRIGGS

Just make up your mind at the very outset that your work is going to stand for quality...that you are going to stamp a superior quality upon everything that goes out of your hands, that whatever you do shall bear the hall-mark of excellence.

ORISON SWETT MARDEN

To feel in our innermost being that we will achieve what we set out to do—this opens the way for miracles. Expecting something to happen energizes our goal and gives it momentum. We often find that life

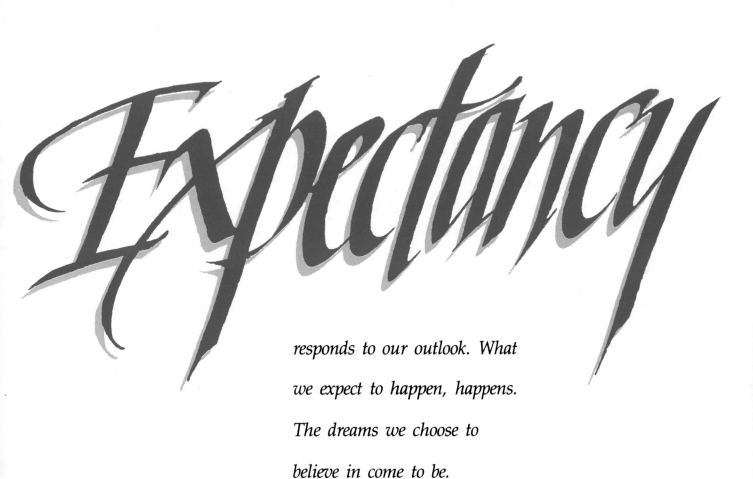

responds to our outlook. What we expect to happen, happens. The dreams we choose to believe in come to be.

Expectancy

We tend to get what we expect.

NORMAN VINCENT PEALE

We usually get what we anticipate....

CLAUDE M. BRISTOL

We find what we expect to find, and we receive what we ask for.

ELBERT HUBBARD

Life is largely a matter of expectation.

HORACE

Life....It tends to respond to our outlook, to shape itself to meet our expectations.

RICHARD M. DeVOS

When you expect things to happen—strangely enough—they do happen.

JOHN J. B. MORGAN and
EWING T. WEBB

Creative power, is that receptive attitude of expectancy which...makes a mould into which the plastic and as yet undifferentiated substance can flow and take the desired form.

THOMAS TROWARD

Your expectation opens or closes the doors of your supply. If you expect grand things, and work honestly for them, they will come to you, your supply will correspond with your expectation.

ORISON SWETT MARDEN

For, he that expects nothing shall not be disappointed, but he that expects much—if he lives and uses that in hand day by day—shall be full to running over.

EDGAR CAYCE

If you paint in your mind a picture of bright and happy expectations, you put yourself into a condition conductive to your goal.

NORMAN VINCENT PEALE

Think and feel yourself there! To achieve any aim in life, you need to project the end-result....Think of the elation, the satisfaction, the joy! Carrying the ecstatic feeling will bring the desired goal into view.

GRACE SPEARE

We advance on our journey only when we face our goal, when we are confident and believe we are going to win out.

ORISON SWETT MARDEN

Sooner or later, those who win are those who think they can.

RICHARD BACH

In order to win, you must expect to win.

DAN FOUTS

Expect victory and you make victory.

PRESTON BRADLEY

If you think you can win, you can win. Faith is necessary to victory.

WILLIAM HAZLITT

Expectancy

He who does not hope to win has already lost.

JOSE JOAQUÍN OLMEDO

Let us choose to believe something good can happen.

J. MARTIN KOHE

There is no medicine like hope, no incentive so great, and no tonic so powerful as expectation of something tomorrow.

ORISON SWETT MARDEN

Hope...is the companion of power, and the mother of success; for whoso hopes strongly has within him the gift of miracles.

SAMUEL SMILES

You begin by always expecting good things to happen.

TOM HOPKINS

Nobody succeeds beyond his or her wildest expectations unless he or she begins with some wild expectations.

RALPH CHARELL

Who asks a king for a penny?

VERNON HOWARD

Successful people are not
afraid to fail. They accept
their failures and continue
on, knowing that failure
is a natural consequence
of trying. They go from

failure to failure, until at
last success is theirs. The
law of failure is one of the
most powerful of all success
laws: we fail only when
we can't accept failure.

Failure

The greatest failure is a person who never admits that he can be a failure.

GERALD N. WEISKOTT

The wise man realistically accepts failures as a part of life and builds a philosophy to meet them and make the most of them. He lives on the principle of "nothing attempted, nothing gained" and is resolved that if he fails he is going to fail while trying to succeed.

WILFERD A. PETERSON

Acceptance of what has happened is the first step to overcoming the consequences of any misfortune.

WILLIAM JAMES

Accept failure as a normal part of living. View it as part of the process of exploring your world; make note of its lessons and move on.

TOM GREENING and DICK HOBSON

You win only if you aren't afraid to lose.

ROCKY AOKI

If you're not big enough to lose, you're not big enough to win.

WALTER REUTHER

True success is overcoming the fear of being unsuccessful.

PAUL SWEENEY

To fail is a natural consequence of trying. To succeed takes time and prolonged effort in the face of unfriendly odds. To think it will be any other way, no matter what you do, is to invite yourself to be hurt and to limit your enthusiasm for trying again.

DAVID VISCOTT

We must expect to fail...but fail in a learning posture, determined not to repeat the mistakes, and to maximize the benefits from what is learned in the process.

TED W. ENGSTROM and
R. ALEC MacKENZIE

It's not easy, but you have to be willing to make mistakes. And the earlier you make those mistakes, the better.

JANE CAHILL PFEIFFER

The difference between greatness and mediocrity is often how an individual views a mistake....

NELSON BOSWELL

The greatest mistake a man can make is to be afraid of making one.

ELBERT HUBBARD

Accept everything about yourself—I mean everything. You are you and that is the beginning and the end—no apologies, no regrets.

CLARK MOUSTAKAS

People who make money often make mistakes, and even have major setbacks, but they believe they will eventually prosper, and they see every setback as a lesson to be applied in their move toward success.

JERRY GILLIES

Failure is success if we learn from it.

MALCOLM S. FORBES

You cannot measure a man by his failures. You must know what use he makes of them. What did they mean to him? What did he get out of them?

ORISON SWETT MARDEN

Failure

There is a wheel on which the affairs of men revolve and its mechanism is such that it prevents any man from being always fortunate.

CROESUS, advisor to Cyrus,
king of the Persians

No man ever achieved worth-while success who did not, at one time or other, find himself with at least one foot hanging well over the brink of failure.

NAPOLEON HILL

We are all of us failures—at least the best of us are.

SIR JAMES M. BARRIE

Forget about the consequences of failure. Failure is only a temporary change in direction to set you straight for your next success.

DENIS E. WAITLEY

No man fails who does his best....

ORISON SWETT MARDEN

Never forget that life can only be nobly inspired and rightly lived if you take it bravely and gallantly, as a splendid adventure in which you are setting out into an unknown country, to face many a danger, to meet many a joy, to find many a comrade, to win and lose many a battle.

ANNIE BESANT

The credit belongs to the man who is actually in the arena; whose face is marred by dust and sweat and blood; who strives valiantly; who errs and comes short again and again; who knows the great enthusiasms, the great devotions, and spends himself in a worthy cause; who at the best knows in the end the triumph of high achievement; and who at the worst, if he fails, at least fails while daring greatly....

THEODORE ROOSEVELT

Faith is based upon
something—the evidence
of things not seen. To
have faith, we must have
evidence. Faith is not blind.
We can know the invisible
by seeing the visible. We can
see the trees bend and know

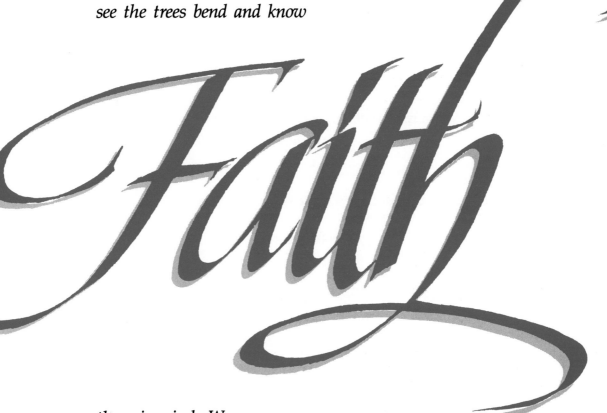

there is wind. We can see
the moon reflect light and
know the sun is shining. We
can see man, and know there
is something beyond.

Faith

It is wrong always, everywhere, and for everyone, to believe anything upon insufficient evidence.

WILLIAM JAMES

Our duty is to believe that for which we have sufficient evidence, and to suspend our judgement when we have not.

JOHN LUBBOCK

It is always right that a man should be able to render a reason for the faith that is within him.

SYDNEY SMITH

Be ready always to give an answer to every man that asketh you a reason of the hope that is in you. . . .

Bible, I PETER 3:15

Faith. . . . Must be enforced by reason. . . . When faith becomes blind it dies.

MOHANDAS GANDHI

The last function of reason is to recognize that there are an infinity of things which surpass it.

BLAISE PASCAL

Faith is not contrary to reason. . . .

SHERWOOD EDDY

Faith is a higher faculty than reason.

HENRY CHRISTOPHER BAILEY

Faith is a continuation of reason.

WILLIAM ADAMS

To mere reason the world always looks two-dimensional.

HERMANN HESSE

The supernatural is the natural not yet understood.

ELBERT HUBBARD

It has been said that a thing is not necessarily against reason, because it happens to be above it.

CHARLES CALEB COLTON

Faith is not belief without proof, but trust without reservations.

ELTON TRUEBLOOD

God does not require you to follow His leading on blind trust. Behold the evidence of an invisible intelligence pervading everything, even your own mind and body.

RAYMOND HOLLIWELL

Faith is...the evidence of things not seen.

Bible, **HEBREWS 11:1**

All that I have seen teaches me to trust the Creator for all I have not seen.

RALPH WALDO EMERSON

The heavens declare the glory of God; and the firmament showeth his handiwork.

Bible, **PSALMS 19:1**

For the invisible things of him from the creation of the world are clearly seen, being understood by the things that are made....

Bible, **ROMANS 1:20**

Faith

I see heaven's glories shine,
And faith shines equal....

EMILY BRONTË

To know what is impenetrable to us really exists,
manifesting itself as the highest wisdom and the
most radiant beauty...this knowledge, this feeling is at
the center of true religiousness.

ALBERT EINSTEIN

The ultimate wisdom which deals with beginnings,
remains locked in a seed. There it lies, the simplest
fact of the universe and at the same time the one which
calls forth faith rather than reason.

HAL BORLAND

The fact that I can plant a seed and it becomes a
flower, share a bit of knowledge and it becomes
another's, smile at someone and receive a smile in return,
are to me continual spiritual exercises.

LEO BUSCAGLIA

They understand but little who understand only what
can be explained.

MARIE EBNER-ESCHENBACH

Man knows much more than he understands.

ALFRED ADLER

No one is going to turn down a good meal because he
does not understand the digestive mechanism.

V. I. KLASSEN

Seek not to understand that you may believe, but
believe that you may understand.

SAINT AUGUSTINE

Some things have to be believed to be seen.

RALPH HODGSON

Vision is the art of seeing things invisible.

JONATHAN SWIFT

We do not need more intellectual power, we need more spiritual power.... We do not need more of the things that are seen, we need more of the things that are unseen.

CALVIN COOLIDGE

Faith is to believe what we do not see; and the reward of this faith is to see what we believe.

SAINT AUGUSTINE

Who has seen the wind?

CHRISTINA ROSSETTI

We shall see but a little way if we require to understand what we see.

HENRY DAVID THOREAU

Faith is power to believe and power to see....

PRENTICE MULFORD

One climbs, one sees. One descends, one sees no longer but one has seen.... When one can no longer see, one can at least still know.

RENÉ DAUMAL

What men have seen they know....

SOPHOCLES

I found Him in the shining of the stars,
I marked Him in the flowering of His fields.

ALFRED LORD TENNYSON

It is only when you are asked to believe in Reason
coming from non-reason that you must cry Halt....
Human minds....They do not come from nowhere.

C. S. LEWIS

I know this world is ruled by infinite intelligence....
Everything that surrounds us—everything that
exists—proves that there are infinite laws behind it.
There can be no denying this fact. It is mathematical
in its precision.

THOMAS A. EDISON

For all his learning or sophistication, man still
instinctively reaches toward that force beyond....
Only arrogance can deny its existence, and the denial
falters in the face of evidence on every hand. In every tuft
of grass, in every bird, in every opening bud, there it is.

HAL BORLAND

The idea of the nest in the bird's mind, where does it
come from?

JOSEPH JOUBERT

The visible marks of extraordinary wisdom and power
appear so plainly in all the works of creation....

JOHN LOCKE

To us also, through every star, through every blade of
grass, is not God made visible if we will open our
minds and our eyes?

THOMAS CARLYLE

Fear is conquered by action.

When we challenge our fears,

we defeat them. When we

Fear

grapple with our difficuties,

they lose their hold upon us.

When we dare to face the

things which scare us, we

open the door to freedom.

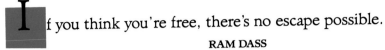

If you think you're free, there's no escape possible.

RAM DASS

There is no liberation without labor...and there is no freedom which is free.

The SIRI SINGH SAHIB

We must be willing to pay a price for freedom....

H. L. MENCKEN

We gain freedom when we have paid the full price....

RABINDRANATH TAGORE

Whatever the price, identify it now. What will you have to go through to get where you want to be?....There is a price you can pay to be free of the situation once and for all. It may be a fantastic price or a tiny one—but there is a price.

HARRY BROWNE

The real price of everything, what everything really costs to the man who wants to acquire it, is the toil and trouble of acquiring it.

ADAM SMITH

Liberty means responsibility.

GEORGE BERNARD SHAW

Those who expect to reap the blessings of freedom, must, like men, undergo the fatigue of supporting it.

THOMAS PAINE

If we wish to free ourselves from enslavement, we must choose freedom and the responsibility this entails.

LEO BUSCAGLIA

We must determine whether we really want freedom—whether we are willing to dare the perils of...rebirth....For we never take a step forward without surrendering something that we may have held dear, without dying to that which has been.

VIRGINIA HANSON

You are free to do whatever you like. You need only face the consequences.

SHELDON KOPP

What is freedom? Freedom is the right to choose: the right to create for oneself the alternatives of choice.

ARCHIBALD MacLEISH

Freedom is the opportunity to make decisions....

KENNETH HILDEBRAND

Freedom is man's capacity to take a hand in his own development. It is our capacity to mold ourselves.

ROLLO MAY

He is free...who knows how to keep in his own hands the power to decide.

SALVADOR DE MADARIAGA

No man is free who is not master of himself.

EPICTETUS

Freedom

The will is never free—it is always attached to an object, a purpose.

JOYCE CARY

Freedom, then, lies only in our innate human capacity to choose between different sorts of bondage, bondage to desire and self esteem, or bondage to the light that lightens all our lives....

SRI MADHAVA ASHISH

Liberty is being free from the things we don't like in order to be slaves of the things we do like.

ERNEST BENN

It is for each of us freely to choose whom we shall serve, and find in that obedience our freedom.

MARY CAROLINE RICHARDS

Riches lie within us, not in material possessions. Our real riches are riches of the head and heart. Satisfaction comes

from appreciating what we have. Wealth without enjoyment is little consolation. Our real prosperity lies in being thankful.

Fulfillment

There are two ways of being happy: we must either diminish our wants or augment our means....

BENJAMIN FRANKLIN

My riches consist not in the extent of my possessions but in the fewness of my wants.

J. BROTHERTON

I would rather be able to appreciate things I can not have than to have things I am not able to appreciate.

ELBERT HUBBARD

Prosperity depends more on wanting what you have than having what you want.

GEOFFRY F. ABERT

Success is getting what you want. Happiness is wanting what you get.

HAYDEN

You have succeeded in life when all you really want is only what you really need.

VERNON HOWARD

What people need and what they want may be very different.

ELBERT HUBBARD

People want riches; they need fulfillment.

BOB CONKLIN

A man should always consider how much he has more than he wants....

JOSEPH ADDISON

It is not the man who has too little, but the man who craves more, that is poor.

SENECA

He is not poor that hath not much, but he that craves much.

THOMAS FULLER

If thou wilt make a man happy, add not unto his riches but take away from his desires.

EPICURUS

He is rich that is satisfied.

THOMAS FULLER

He who is contented is rich.

LAO-TZU

He is richest who is content with the least....

SOCRATES

That man is richest whose pleasures are the cheapest.

HENRY DAVID THOREAU

A man is rich in proportion to the number of things he can afford to let alone.

HENRY DAVID THOREAU

Who is rich? He that rejoices in his portion.

BENJAMIN FRANKLIN

Remember this—that very little is needed to make a happy life.

MARCUS AURELIUS

139

Fulfillment

Nothing is enough for the man to whom enough is too little.

EPICURUS

He who knows that enough is enough will always have enough.

LAO-TZU

He is a wise man who does not grieve for the things which he has not, but rejoices for those which he has.

EPICTETUS

He who is plenteously provided for from within, needs but little from without.

JOHANN WOLFGANG VON GOETHE

It is not how much we have, but how much we enjoy. . . .

CHARLES H. SPURGEON

Not what we have,
But what we enjoy
Constitutes our abundance.

J. PETIT-SENN

Wealth is not his that has it, but his that enjoys it.

BENJAMIN FRANKLIN

He enjoys much who is thankful for little.

THOMAS SECKER

Don't complain because you don't have. . . . Enjoy what you've got. . . .

H. STANLEY JUDD

Let not your mind run on what you lack as much as on what you have already.

MARCUS AURELIUS

Where a man can live, he can also live well....

MARCUS AURELIUS

I have learned, in whatsoever state I am, therewith to be content.

Bible, PHILIPPIANS 4:11

My crown is in my heart, not on my head,
Nor decked with diamonds and Indian stones,
Nor to be seen: My crown is called content;
A crown it is, that seldom kings enjoy.

WILLIAM SHAKESPEARE

The man who has no money is poor, but one who has nothing but money is poorer. He only is rich who can enjoy without owning; he is poor who though he have millions is covetous.

ORISON SWETT MARDEN

There's a basic human weakness inherent in all people which tempts them to want what they can't have and not want what is readily available to them.

ROBERT J. RINGER

Getting anything changes it from being desirable to just being taken for granted.

UNKNOWN

Money never made a man happy yet, nor will it.... The more a man has, the more he wants. Instead of filling a vacuum, it makes one.

BENJAMIN FRANKLIN

Fulfillment

Riches rather enlarge than satisfy appetites.

THOMAS FULLER

He who multiplies riches multiplies cares.

BENJAMIN FRANKLIN

A great fortune is a great slavery.

SENECA

Gold will be either slave or master.

HORACE

Money is a good servant, but a poor master.

DOMINIQUE BOUHOURS

He does not possess wealth that allows it to possess him.

BENJAMIN FRANKLIN

The victor belongs to the spoils.

F. SCOTT FITZGERALD

That glittering hope is immemorial and beckons many men to their undoing.

EURIPIDES

Success has made failures of many men.

CINDY ADAMS

Don't forget until too late that the business of life is not business, but living.

B. C. FORBES

There is a serious defect in the thinking of someone who wants—more than anything else—to become rich. As long as they don't have the money, it'll seem like a worthwhile goal. Once they do, they'll understand how important other things are—and have always been.

JOSEPH BROOKS

There is a time when a man distinguishes the idea of felicity from the idea of wealth; it is the beginning of wisdom.

RALPH WALDO EMERSON

Money cannot buy peace of mind. It cannot heal ruptured relationships, or build meaning into a life that has none.

RICHARD M. DeVOS

The only thing money gives you is the freedom of not worrying about money.

JOHNNY CARSON

The use of money is all the advantage there is in having it.

BENJAMIN FRANKLIN

A rich man is nothing but a poor man with money.

W. C. FIELDS

A man's life consisteth not in the abundance of the things which he possesseth.

Bible, LUKE 12:15

The quality of life is in the mind, not in material.

MALCOLM S. FORBES

Fulfillment

It is the heart that makes a man rich. He is rich according to what he is, not according to what he has.

HENRY WARD BEECHER

Joy is not in things, it is in us.

RICHARD WAGNER

I have enough to eat and wear, and time to see how beautiful the world is, and to enjoy it.

JOHN BURROUGHS

Everything that's really worthwhile in life comes to us free.

EARL NIGHTINGALE

The best things in life are free.

LEW BROWN and BUDDY DE SYLVA

The best things in life aren't things.

RAVEN

There is no wealth but life.

JOHN RUSKIN

The only wealth is life.

HENRY DAVID THOREAU

What power can poverty have over a home where loving hearts are beating with a consciousness of untold riches of the head and heart?

ORISON SWETT MARDEN

It's a universal law—we have
to give before we get. We must
plant the seeds before we reap

the harvest. The more we sow,
the more we reap. And in
giving to others, we find
ourselves blessed. The law
works to give us back more
than we have sown. The
giver's harvest is always full.

Giving

To get, give.

BOB ROTH

You give before you get.

NAPOLEON HILL

To give is to receive....

GERALD G. JAMPOLSKY

Giving opens the way for receiving.

FLORENCE SCOVEL SHINN

You must give to get. You must sow the seed, before you can reap the harvest.

SCOTT REED

The liberal soul shall be made fat: and he that watereth shall be watered also himself.

Bible, PROVERBS 11:25

You have to sow before you can reap. You have to give before you can get.

ROBERT COLLIER

When you give yourself, you receive more than you give.

ANTOINE DE SAINT-EXUPERY

There never was a person who did anything worth doing that did not receive more than he gave.

HENRY WARD BEECHER

Plant a kernel of wheat and you reap a pint; plant a pint, and you reap a bushel. Always the law works to give you back more than you give.

ANTHONY NORVELL

There would be no advantage to be gained by sowing a field of wheat if the harvest did not return more than was sown.

NAPOLEON HILL

The law of harvest is to reap more than you sow.

GEORGE DANA BOARDMAN

The best thing about giving of ourselves is that what we get is always better than what we give. The reaction is greater than the action.

ORISON SWETT MARDEN

It is more blessed to give than to receive.

Bible, ACTS 20:35

For it is in giving that we receive.

SAINT FRANCIS OF ASSISI

Give, and it shall be given unto you: good measure, pressed down, and shaken together, and running over....

Bible, LUKE 6:38

It is like the seed put into the soil—the more one sows, the greater the harvest.

ORISON SWETT MARDEN

Sow much, reap much; sow little, reap little.

CHINESE PROVERB

Giving

The more we give of anything, the more we shall get back.

GRACE SPEARE

We must give more in order to get more. It is the generous giving of ourselves that produces the generous harvest.

ORISON SWETT MARDEN

The gifts that one receives for giving are so immeasurable that it is almost an injustice to accept them.

ROD McKUEN

For true love is inexhaustible: the more you give, the more you have. And if you go to draw at the true fountainhead, the more water you draw, the more abundant is its flow.

ANTOINE DE SAINT-EXUPERY

This is the miracle that happens every time to those who really love: the more they give, the more they possess....

RAINER MARIA RILKE

One man gives freely, yet grows all the richer; another withholds what he should give, and only suffers want.

Bible, PROVERBS 11:24

Getters don't get—givers get.

EUGENE BENGE

He who obtains has little. He who scatters has much.

LAO-TZU

ature does not give to those who will not spend....

R. J. BAUGHAN

he evidence unmistakably indicates that you have to spend money in order to make money.

SRULLY BLOTNICK

have always noticed that the man who gives the most for the money, gets the most business.

VASH YOUNG

he man who will use his skill and constructive imagination to see how much he can give for a dollar, instead of how little he can give for a dollar, is bound to succeed.

HENRY FORD

ny person who contributes to prosperity must prosper in turn.

EARL NIGHTINGALE

n helping others, we shall help ourselves, for whatever good we give out completes the circle and comes back to us.

FLORA EDWARDS

en are rich only as they give. He who gives great service gets great returns.

ELBERT HUBBARD

ot he who has much is rich, but he who gives much.

ERICH FROMM

Giving

You only get to keep what you give away.

SHELDON KOPP

What you keep to yourself you lose, what you give away,
you keep forever.

MUNTHE

What we gave, we have;
What we spent, we had;
What we left, we lost.

Inscription, tomb of
EDWARD (THE GOOD)

Nothing that you have not given away will ever be
really yours.

C. S. LEWIS

You cannot hold on to anything good. You must be
continually giving—and getting. You cannot hold on
to your seed. You must sow it—and reap anew. You cannot
hold on to riches. You must use them and get other riches
in return.

ROBERT COLLIER

Look around for a place to sow a few seeds....

HENRY VAN DYKE

A handful of pine-seed will cover mountains with the
green majesty of forests. I too will set my face to the
wind and throw my handful of seed on high.

FIONA MacLEOD (William Sharp)

The purpose of goals is to focus our attention. The mind will not reach toward achievement

Goals

until it has clear objectives. The magic begins when we set goals. It is then that the switch is turned on, the current begins to flow, and the power to accomplish becomes a reality.

Goals

There are those who travel and those who are going somewhere. They are different and yet they are the same. The success has this over his rivals: he knows where he is going.

MARK CAINE

The first essential, of course, is to know what you want.

ROBERT COLLIER

The most important thing about goals is having one.

GEOFFRY F. ABERT

The big thing is that you know what you want.

EARL NIGHTINGALE

There is one quality which one must possess to win, and that is definiteness of purpose, the knowledge of what one wants, and a burning desire to possess it.

NAPOLEON HILL

The indispensable first step to getting the things you want out of life is this: decide what you want.

BEN STEIN

In whatever position you find yourself determine first your objective.

MARSHAL FERDINAND FOCH

Until input (thought) is linked to a goal (purpose) there can be no intelligent accomplishment.

PAUL G. THOMAS

A set definite objective must be established if we are to accomplish anything in a big way.

JOHN McDONALD

There is no achievement without goals.

ROBERT J. McKAIN

This one step—choosing a goal and sticking to it—changes everything.

SCOTT REED

People with goals succeed because they know where they're going.

EARL NIGHTINGALE

If you don't know where you are going, how can you expect to get there?

BASIL S. WALSH

You are not likely to get anywhere in particular if you don't know where you want to go.

PERCY H. JOHNSON

If you don't know where you are going, any road will get you there.

UNKNOWN

If a man knows not what harbor he seeks, any wind is the right wind.

SENECA

No wind serves him who addresses his voyage to no certain port.

MICHEL EYQUEM DE MONTAIGNE

Goals

A man without a purpose is like a ship without a rudder.

THOMAS CARLYLE

If you don't know where you are going, you will probably end up somewhere else.

LAURENCE J. PETER

Without a goal to work toward, we will not get there.

NATASHA JOSEFOWITZ

'Would you tell me, please, which way I ought to go from here?'
'That depends a good deal on where you want to get to,' said the Cat.
'I don't much care where—' said Alice.
'Then it doesn't matter which way you go,' said the Cat.

LEWIS CARROLL, Alice's
Adventures in Wonderland

It is hard to begin to move when you don't know where you are moving, how to move, or if you are going to get there.

PETER NIVIO ZARLENGA

You return and again take the proper course, guided by what?—By the picture in mind of the place you are headed for....

JOHN McDONALD

Knowing where you're going is all you need to get there.

CARL FREDERICK

The world has the habit of making room for the man whose words and actions show that he knows where he is going.

NAPOLEON HILL

Those who cannot tell what they desire or expect still sigh and struggle with indefinite thoughts and vast wishes.

RALPH WALDO EMERSON

The world turns aside to let any man pass who knows whither he is going.

DAVID STARR JORDAN

If we could first know where we are, and whither we are tending, we could better judge what to do and how to do it.

ABRAHAM LINCOLN

What an immense power over the life is the power of possessing distinct aims. The voice, the dress, the look, the very motions of a person, define and alter when he or she begins to live for a reason.

ELIZABETH STUART PHELPS

If I've got correct goals, and if I keep pursuing them the best way I know how, everything else falls into line. If I do the right thing right, I'm going to succeed.

DAN DIERDORF

We are what and where we are because we have first imagined it....

DONALD CURTIS

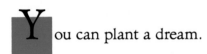

Goals

Y-ou will now have a starting place and a destination, and you will be able to determine what it will cost you to get there.... You will be going someplace.

H. STANLEY JUDD

Y-ou, too, can determine what you want. You can decide on your major objectives, targets, aims, and destination.

W. CLEMENT STONE

Y-ou can plant a dream.

ANNE CAMPBELL

Growth is the process of

responding positively to change.

Grappling with hardships,

trouble, and calamity; facing

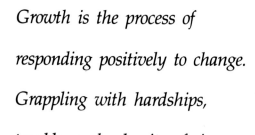

adversity in a spirit of

determination and courage;

loving and not being crushed

by broken hopes; holding our

head high, having done our

best—this is growth.

Honesty

To every man there openeth
A way, and ways, and a way.
And the high soul climbs the high way,
And the low soul gropes the low:
And in between, on the misty flats,
The rest drift to and fro.
But to every man there openeth
A high way and a low,
And every man decideth
The way his soul shall go.

JOHN OXENHAM

Any path is only a path. There is no affront to yourself or others in dropping it if that is what your heart tells you to do. But your decision to keep on the path or to leave it must be free of fear and ambition. I warn you: look at every path closely and deliberately. Try it as many times as you think necessary. Then ask yourself and yourself alone one question. It is this: Does the path have a heart? . . . . Does this path have a heart is the only question. If it does, then the path is good. If it doesn't, it is of no use.

CARLOS CASTANEDA

The essence of greatness is the perception that virtue is enough.

RALPH WALDO EMERSON

Honesty is the first chapter of the book of wisdom.

THOMAS JEFFERSON

He is not great who is not greatly good.

WILLIAM SHAKESPEARE

They're only truly great who are truly good.

GEORGE CHAPMAN

Growth is the process of
responding positively to change.
Grappling with hardships,
trouble, and calamity; facing

Growth

adversity in a spirit of
determination and courage;
loving and not being crushed
by broken hopes; holding our
head high, having done our
best—this is growth.

Growth

Growth means change and change involves risks, stepping from the known to the unknown.

GEORGE SHINN

We grow because we struggle, we learn and overcome.

R. C. ALLEN

Strength and growth come only through continuous effort and struggle....

NAPOLEON HILL

All growth depends upon activity. There is no development...without effort....Work is...the only means to manhood....

CALVIN COOLIDGE

Difficulties are the things that show what men are.

EPICTETUS

It cannot be too often repeated that it is not helps, but obstacles, not facilities, but difficulties that make men.

WILLIAM MATHEWS

Men...are bettered and improved by trial, and refined out of broken hopes and blighted expectations.

F. W. ROBERTSON

He that wrestles with us strengthens our nerves and sharpens our skill. Our antagonist is our helper.

EDMUND BURKE

All life demands struggle. Those who have everything given to them become lazy, selfish, and insensitive to the real values of life. The very striving and hard work that we so constantly try to avoid is the major building block in the person we are today.

RALPH RANSOM

Out of love and hatred, out of earnings and borrowings and leadings and losses; out of sickness and pain; out of wooing and worshipping; out of traveling and voting and watching and caring; out of disgrace and contempt, comes our tuition in the serene and beautiful laws.

RALPH WALDO EMERSON

He who knows no hardships will know no hardihood. He who faces no calamity will need no courage. Mysterious though it is, the characteristics in human nature which we love best grow in a soil with a strong mixture of troubles.

HARRY EMERSON FOSDICK

Trouble is the common denominator of living. It is the great equalizer.

ANN LANDERS

The very greatest things—great thoughts, discoveries, inventions—have usually been nurtured in hardship, often pondered over in sorrow, and at length established with difficulty.

SAMUEL SMILES

The apprenticeship of difficulty is one which the greatest of men have had to serve.

SAMUEL SMILES

Our trials, our sorrows, and our griefs develop us....

ORISON SWETT MARDEN

Growth

The work of many of the greatest men, inspired by duty, has been done amidst suffering and trial and difficulty. They have struggled against the tide, and reached the shore exhausted....

SAMUEL SMILES

Yet learned he obedience by the things which he suffered....

Bible, HEBREWS 5:8

Troubles are often the tools by which God fashions us for better things.

HENRY WARD BEECHER

We were promised sufferings. They were part of the program. We were even told, "Blessed are they that mourn"....

C. S. LEWIS

A grindstone that had not grit in it, how long would it take to sharpen an axe? And affairs that had not grit in them, how long would they take to make a man?

HENRY WARD BEECHER

The gem cannot be polished without friction, nor man perfected without trials.

CHINESE PROVERB

Sooner or later comes a crisis in our affairs, and how we meet it determines our future happiness and success. Since the beginning of time, every form of life has been called upon to meet such crisis.

ROBERT COLLIER

Close scrutiny will show that most..."crisis situations" are...opportunities to either advance, or stay where you are.

MAXWELL MALTZ

What happens is not as important as how you react to what happens.

THADDEUS GOLAS

When something (an affliction) happens to you, you either let it defeat you, or you defeat it....

ROSALIND RUSSELL

A man either lives life as it happens to him, meets it head-on and licks it, or he turns his back on it and starts to wither away.

GENE RODDENBERRY

In the final analysis, the questions of why bad things happen to good people transmutes itself into some very different questions, no longer asking why something happened, but asking how we will respond, what we intend to do now that it has happened.

HAROLD S. KUSHNER

Am I willing to give up what I have in order to be what I am not yet?....Am I able to follow the spirit of love into the desert?....It is a frightening and sacred moment. There is no return. One's life is changed forever. It is the fire that gives us our shape.

MARY CAROLINE RICHARDS

Fire is the test of gold; adversity, of strong men.

SENECA

Growth

For gold is tried in the fire and acceptable men in the furnace of adversity.

SIRACH

Behold, I have refined thee, but not with silver; I have chosen thee in the furnace of affliction.

Bible, ISAIAH 48:10

The proof of gold is fire....

BENJAMIN FRANKLIN

They that sow in tears shall reap in joy.

Bible, PSALMS 126:5

Before the reward there must be labor. You plant before you harvest. You sow in tears before you reap in joy.

RALPH RANSOM

It is easy enough to be pleasant,
When life flows by like a song,
But the man worth while is the one who can smile,
When everything goes dead wrong.
For the test of the heart is trouble,
And it always comes with the years,
And the smile that is worth the praises of earth
Is the smile that shines through tears.

ELLA WHEELER WILCOX

I have always believed, and I still believe, that whatever good or bad fortune may come our way we can always give it meaning and transform it into something of value.

HERMANN HESSE

I believe that all that we go through here must have some value.

ELEANOR ROOSEVELT

Life is my college.

LOUISA MAY ALCOTT

Life is a classroom in which each of us is being tested, tried, and passed.

ROBERT THIBODEAU

We must accept life for what it actually is—a challenge to our quality without which we should never know of what stuff we are made, or grow to our full stature.

I. A. R. WYLIE

The mere fact that you have obstacles to overcome is in your favor....

ROBERT COLLIER

However mean your life is, meet it and live it; do not shun it and call it hard names. It is not so bad as you are. It looks poorest when you are the richest.

HENRY DAVID THOREAU

Only when we are no longer afraid do we begin to live....

DOROTHY THOMPSON

Events will take their course, it is no good our being angry at them; he is happiest who wisely turns them to the best account.

EURIPIDES

Growth

I exhort you also to take part in the great combat, which is the combat of life, and greater than every other earthly conflict.

PLATO

If this life be not a real fight, in which something is eternally gained...it is no better than a game of private theatricals from which one may withdraw at will.

WILLIAM JAMES

There are obstinate and unknown braves who defend themselves inch by inch in the shadows against the fatal invasion of want and turpitude. There are noble and mysterious triumphs which no eye sees, no renown rewards, and no flourish of trumpets salutes. Life, misfortune, isolation, abandonment, and poverty are battlefields which have their heroes.

VICTOR HUGO

Life is a series of experiences, each one of which makes us bigger, even though sometimes it is hard to realize this. For the world was built to develop character, and we must learn that the setbacks and griefs which we endure help us in our marching onward.

HENRY FORD

March on. Do not tarry. To go forward is to move toward perfection. March on, and fear not the thorns, or the sharp stones on life's path.

KAHLIL GIBRAN

God will not look you over for medals, degrees or diplomas, but for scars.

ELBERT HUBBARD

Every winner has scars.

HERBERT N. CASSON

There are no winners, only survivors.

FRANK GIFFORD

I am a frayed and nibbled survivor in a fallen world, and I am getting along. I am aging and eaten and have done my share of eating too. I am not washed and beautiful, in control of a shining world in which everything fits, but instead am wandering awed about on a splintered wreck I've come to care for, whose gnawed trees breathe a delicate air, whose bloodied and scarred creatures are my dearest companions, and whose beauty beats and shines not in its imperfections but overwhelmingly in spite of them....

ANNIE DILLARD

I am convinced that the world is not a mere bog in which men and women trample themselves in the mire and die. Something magnificent is taking place here amid the cruelties and tragedies, and the supreme challenge to intelligence is that of making the noblest and best in our curious heritage prevail.

CHARLES A. BEARD

The sculptor will chip off all unnecessary material to set free the angel. Nature will chip and pound us remorselessly to bring out our possibilities. She will strip us of wealth, humble our pride, humiliate our ambition, let us down from the ladder of fame, will discipline us in a thousand ways, if she can develop a little character. Everything must give way to that. Wealth is nothing, position is nothing, fame is nothing, manhood is everything.

ORISON SWETT MARDEN

Each experience through which we pass operates ultimately for our good.... This is a correct attitude to adopt... and we must be able to see it in that light.

RAYMOND HOLLIWELL

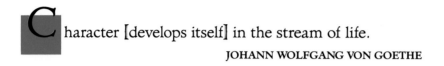

Growth

Character is a mark cut upon something, and this indelible mark determines the only true value of all people and all their work.

ORISON SWETT MARDEN

Character [develops itself] in the stream of life.

JOHANN WOLFGANG VON GOETHE

The highest qualities of character...must be earned.

LYMAN ABBOTT

Therefore keep in the midst of life. Do not isolate yourself. Be among men and things, and among troubles, and difficulties, and obstacles.

HENRY DRUMMOND

I think of those who were truly great.
The names of those who in their lives fought for life,
Who wore at their hearts the fire's centre.

STEPHEN SPENDER

We cannot tell what may happen to us in the strange medley of life. But we can decide what happens in us—how we can take it, what we do with it—and that is what really counts in the end. How to take the raw stuff of life and make it a thing of worth and beauty—that is the test of living.

JOSEPH FORT NEWTON

The force of habit can be swift
to push us to failure or to
success. The more we do
something, the more likely we
are to do it again. Habit is like
a cable—coiled, it binds us as

its slave; stretched like a bridge,
it enables us to walk across the
deepest valley to freedom.

Habit

Habit is a form of exercise.

ELBERT HUBBARD

Habit, my friend, is practice long pursued, that at last becomes the man himself.

EVENUS

We are what we repeatedly do.

ARISTOTLE

The more deeply the path is etched, the more it is used, and the more it is used, the more deeply it is etched.

JO COUDERT

The more one works, the more willing one is to work.

LORD CHESTERFIELD

The harder you work, the harder it is to surrender.

VINCE LOMBARDI

Once in motion, a pattern tends to stay in motion.

J. G. GALLIMORE

The easier it is to do, the harder it is to change.

ENG'S PRINCIPLE

The beginning of a habit is like an invisible thread, but every time we repeat the act we strengthen the strand, add to it another filament, until it becomes a great cable and binds us irrevocably thought and act.

ORISON SWETT MARDEN

Any act often repeated soon forms a habit; and habit allowed, steadily gains in strength. At first it may be but as a spider's web, easily broken through, but if not resisted it soon binds us with chains of steel.

TRYON EDWARDS

There is an invisible garment woven around us from our earliest years; it is made of the way we eat, the way we walk, the way we greet people....

JEAN GIRAUDOUX

Habit is a cable; we weave a thread of it each day, and at last we cannot break it.

HORACE MANN

We first make our habits, and then our habits make us.

JOHN DRYDEN

As the twig is bent the tree inclines.

VIRGIL

Man becomes a slave to his constantly repeated acts.... What he at first chooses, at last compels.

ORISON SWETT MARDEN

The individual who wants to reach the top in business must appreciate the might of the force of habit—and must understand that practices are what create habits. He must be quick to break those habits that can break him— and hasten to adopt those practices that will become the habits that help him achieve the success he desires.

J. PAUL GETTY

Habit is either the best of servants or the worst of masters.

NATHANIEL EMMONS

Habit

"How shall I a habit break?"
As you did that habit make.
As you gathered, you must lose;
As you yielded, now refuse.
Thread by thread the strands we twist
Till they bind us neck and wrist.
Thread by thread the patient hand
Must untwine ere free we stand.

JOHN BOYLE O'REILLY

Habits....the only reason they persist is that they are offering some satisfaction....You allow them to persist by not seeking any other, better form of satisfying the same needs. Every habit, good or bad, is acquired and learned in the same way—by finding that it is a means of satisfaction.

JULIENE BERK

Our repeated failures to fully act as we would wish must not discourage us. It is the sincere intention that is the essential thing, and this will in time release us from the bondage of habits which at present seem almost insuperable.

THOMAS TROWARD

Thoughts lead on to purposes; purposes go forth in action; action form habits; habits decide character; and character fixes our destiny.

TRYON EDWARDS

Sow an act...reap a habit;
Sow a habit...reap a character;
Sow a character...reap a destiny.

GEORGE DANA BOARDMAN

*We are happy when we are
using our potential. Striving
against difficulties and*

*overcoming them—reaching for
achievement and finding it—
this is happiness. We are happy
when we are learning, growing,
and accomplishing. Working
toward a worthy goal that
demands our best is the secret
of happiness.*

Happiness

Joy comes from using your potential.

WILL SCHULTZ

True happiness involves the full use of one's powers and talents.

JOHN W. GARDNER

Happiness is the full use of your powers along lines of excellence in a life affording scope.

JOHN F. KENNEDY

The truth is that all of us attain the greatest success and happiness possible in this life whenever we use our native capacities to their greatest extent.

SMILEY BLANTON

Such happiness as life is capable of comes from the full participation of all our powers in the endeavor to wrest from each changing situation of experience its own full and unique meaning.

JOHN DEWEY

Happiness includes chiefly the idea of satisfaction after full honest effort. No one can possibly be satisfied and no one can be happy who feels that in some paramount affair he has failed to take up the challenge of life.

ARNOLD BENNETT

This is the true joy of life—the being used for a purpose recognized by yourself as a mighty one, the being thoroughly worn out before you are thrown to the scrap-heap....

GEORGE BERNARD SHAW

Happiness does not come from doing easy work but from the afterglow of satisfaction that comes after the achievement of a difficult task that demanded our best.

THEODORE I. RUBIN

The glow of satisfaction which follows the consciousness of doing our level best never comes to a human being from any other experience.

ORISON SWETT MARDEN

True happiness comes from the joy of deeds well done, the zest of creating things new.

ANTOINE DE SAINT-EXUPÉRY

There is no greater joy than that of feeling oneself a creator. The triumph of life is expressed by creation.

HENRI BERGSON

It is in the compelling zest of high adventure and of victory, and in creative action, that man finds his supreme joys.

ANTOINE DE SAINT-EXUPÉRY

What a man really wants is creative challenge with sufficient skills to bring him within the reach of success so that he may have the expanding joy of achievement.

FAY B. NASH

Happiness...it lies in the joy of achievement, in the thrill of creative effort.

FRANKLIN DELANO ROOSEVELT

The human spirit needs to accomplish, to achieve, to triumph to be happy.

BEN STEIN

Happiness

Satisfaction lies in the effort, not in the attainment. Full effort is full victory.

MOHANDAS GANDHI

Happiness is not pleasure, it is victory.

ZIG ZIGLAR

Happiness is neither virtue nor pleasure nor this thing nor that but simply growth. We are happy when we are growing.

WILLIAM BUTLER YEATS

Growth itself contains the germ of happiness.

PEARL S. BUCK

Do you want my one-word secret of happiness? It's growth—mental, financial, you name it.

HAROLD S. GENEEN

Happiness is a by-product. You cannot pursue it by itself.

SAMUEL LEVENSON

We are built to conquer environment, solve problems, achieve goals, and we find no real satisfaction or happiness in life without obstacles to conquer and goals to achieve.

MAXWELL MALTZ

Happiness requires problems....

H. L. HOLLINGWORTH

To strive with difficulties, and to conquer them, is the highest human felicity.

SAMUEL JOHNSON

One might think that the money value of an invention constitutes its reward to the man who loves his work. But, speaking for myself, I can honestly say this is not so....I continue to find my greatest pleasure, and so my reward, in the work that precedes what the world calls success.

THOMAS A. EDISON

We find greatest joy, not in getting, but in expressing what we are....Men do not really live for honors or for pay; their gladness is not in the taking and holding, but in the doing, the striving, the building, the living. It is a higher joy to teach than to be taught. It is good to get justice, but better to do it; fun to have things but more to make them. The happy man is he who lives the life of love, not for the honors it may bring, but for the life itself.

R. J. BAUGHAN

There is joy in work....There is no happiness except in the realization that we have accomplished something.

HENRY FORD

The mintage of wisdom is to know that rest is rust, and that real life is love, laughter, and work.

ELBERT HUBBARD

Happiness consists in activity. It is a running stream, not a stagnant pool.

JOHN MASON GOOD

Happiness is not in having or being; it is in doing.

LILIAN EICHLER WATSON

The secret of happiness is something to do.

JOHN BURROUGHS

Happiness

The soul's joy lies in doing.

PERCY BYSSHE SHELLEY

The enjoyment of life would be instantly gone if you removed the possibility of doing something.

CHAUNCEY M. DEPEW

Action itself, so long as I am convinced that it is right action, gives me satisfaction.

JAWAHARLAL NEHRU

A mind always employed is always happy. This is the true secret, the grand recipe, for felicity.

THOMAS JEFFERSON

If you observe a really happy man you will find him building a boat, writing a symphony, educating his son, growing Double Dahlias in his garden.

W. BERAN WOLFE

Happiness…she loves to see men at work. She loves sweat, weariness, self sacrifice. She will be found not in palaces but lurking in cornfields and factories; and hovering over littered desks; she crowns the unconscious head of the busy child.

DAVID GRAYSON

Now and then a wearied king, or a tormented slave, found out where the true kingdoms of the world were, and possessed himself in a furrow or two of garden ground, of truly infinite dominion.

JOHN RUSKIN

Yes, there is a nirvana; it is in leading your sheep to a green pasture, and in putting your child to sleep, and in writing the last line of your poem.

KAHLIL GIBRAN

Before us lie two paths—

honesty and dishonesty. The

shortsighted embark on the

dishonest path; the wise on the

honest. For the wise know the

truth: in helping others we

help ourselves; and in hurting

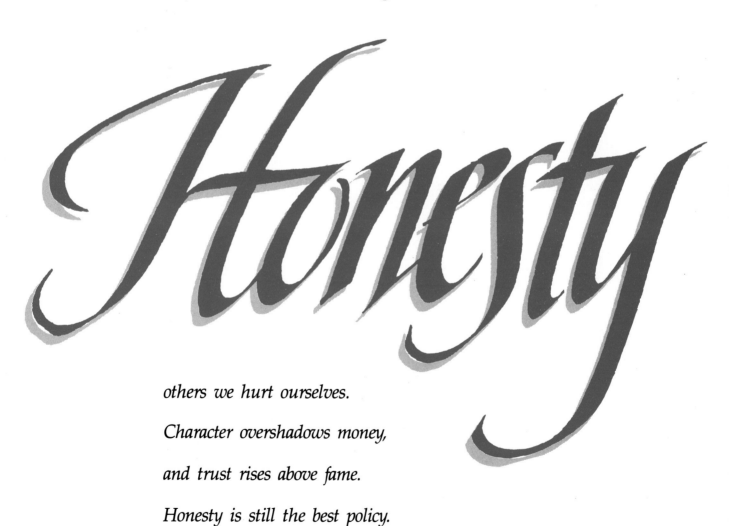

others we hurt ourselves.

Character overshadows money,

and trust rises above fame.

Honesty is still the best policy.

Honesty

Good thoughts bear good fruit, bad thoughts bear bad fruit.

JAMES ALLEN

Understand this law and you will then know, beyond room for the slightest doubt, that you are constantly punishing yourself for every wrong you commit and rewarding yourself for every act of constructive conduct in which you indulge.

NAPOLEON HILL

It is an enduring truth, which can never be altered, that every infraction of the Law of Nature must carry its punitive consequences with it. We can never get beyond the range of cause and effect.

THOMAS TROWARD

Everyone will experience the consequences of his own acts. If his acts are right, he'll get good consequences; if they're not, he'll suffer for it.

HARRY BROWNE

Sooner or later everyone sits down to a banquet of consequences.

ROBERT LOUIS STEVENSON

Whatever our creed, we feel that no good deed can by any possibility go unrewarded, no evil deed unpunished.

ORISON SWETT MARDEN

You cannot do wrong without suffering wrong.

RALPH WALDO EMERSON

Every act of virtue is an ingredient unto reward.

JEREMY TAYLOR

Each time you are honest and conduct yourself with honesty, a success force will drive you toward greater success. Each time you lie, even with a little white lie, there are strong forces pushing you toward failure.

JOSEPH SUGARMAN

It is better to be defeated on principle than to win on lies.

ARTHUR CALWELL

Rather fail with honor than succeed by fraud.

SOPHOCLES

The darkest hour of any man's life is when he sits down to plan how to get money without earning it.

HORACE GREELEY

Prefer a loss to a dishonest gain; the one brings pain at the moment, the other for all time.

CHILON

It is better to deserve honors and not have them than to have them and not deserve them.

MARK TWAIN

You can never lose anything that really belongs to you, and you can't keep that which belongs to someone else.

EDGAR CAYCE

There is no right way to do something wrong.

UNKNOWN

Honesty

You can't make wrong work.

GERALD WATERHOUSE

We can cure these failure symptoms, not by will power, but by understanding—by being able to "see" that they do not work and that they are inappropriate. The truth can set us free from them.

MAXWELL MALTZ

Morality may consist solely in the courage of making a choice.

LÉON BLUM

To many a man, and sometimes to a youth, there comes the opportunity to choose between honorable competence and tainted wealth....The young man who starts out to be poor and honorable, holds in his hand one of the strongest elements of success.

ORISON SWETT MARDEN

It is the eternal struggle between these two principles—right and wrong....They are the two principles that have stood face to face from the beginning of time and will ever continue to struggle....It is the same spirit that says, "You work and toil and earn bread, and I'll eat it."

ABRAHAM LINCOLN

There are two great forces in this world—good and evil; and no man is worth his salt unless he has lost and won battles for a principle.

A. P. GOUTHEY

There are always two choices. Two paths to take. One is easy. And its only reward is that it's easy.

UNKNOWN

It is easy to hate and it is difficult to love. This is how the whole scheme of things works. All good things are difficult to achieve; and bad things are very easy to get.

MORARJI DESAI

Badness you can get easily, in quantity: the road is smooth, and it lies close by. But in front of excellence the immortal gods have put sweat, and long and steep is the way to it.

HESIOD

The path is smooth that leadeth on to danger.

WILLIAM SHAKESPEARE

Honors are easier had than honor.

MALCOLM S. FORBES

Wickedness is always easier than virtue, for it takes a short cut to everything.

SAMUEL JOHNSON

Once to every man and nation comes
The moment to decide,
In the strife of Truth and Falsehood,
For the good or evil side.

JAMES RUSSELL LOWELL

Refuse the evil, and choose the good.

Bible, ISAIAH 7:15

I have set before you life and death, blessing and cursing: therefore choose life....

Bible, DEUTERONOMY 30:19

Honesty

To every man there openeth
A way, and ways, and a way.
And the high soul climbs the high way,
And the low soul gropes the low:
And in between, on the misty flats,
The rest drift to and fro.
But to every man there openeth
A high way and a low,
And every man decideth
The way his soul shall go.

JOHN OXENHAM

Any path is only a path. There is no affront to yourself or others in dropping it if that is what your heart tells you to do. But your decision to keep on the path or to leave it must be free of fear and ambition. I warn you: look at every path closely and deliberately. Try it as many times as you think necessary. Then ask yourself and yourself alone one question. It is this: Does the path have a heart?.... Does this path have a heart is the only question. If it does, then the path is good. If it doesn't, it is of no use.

CARLOS CASTANEDA

The essence of greatness is the perception that virtue is enough.

RALPH WALDO EMERSON

Honesty is the first chapter of the book of wisdom.

THOMAS JEFFERSON

He is not great who is not greatly good.

WILLIAM SHAKESPEARE

They're only truly great who are truly good.

GEORGE CHAPMAN

There is something greater than wealth, grander even than fame—...manhood, character, stand for success...nothing else really does.

ORISON SWETT MARDEN

No legacy is so rich as honesty.

WILLIAM SHAKESPEARE

It is possible that the scrupulously honest man may not grow rich so fast as the unscrupulous and dishonest one; but the success will be of a truer kind, earned without fraud or injustice. And even though a man should for a time be unsuccessful, still he must be honest: better lose all and save character. For character is itself a fortune....

SAMUEL SMILES

Who can estimate the real wealth that inheres in a fine character....How base and mean money and huge estates look in comparison. All other things fade before it. Its touch is like magic to win friendship, influence, power. Can you afford to chill, to discourage, to crush out of your life this sweet, sensitive plant, which would flower in your nature and give added glory to your life, for the sake of a few dollars, a little questionable fame?

ORISON SWETT MARDEN

If we put the emphasis upon the right things, if we live the life that is worth while, and then fail, we will survive all disasters, we will out-live all misfortune. We should be so well balanced and symmetrical, that nothing which could ever happen could throw us off our center, so that no matter what misfortune should overtake us, there would still be a whole magnificent man or woman left after being stripped of everything else.

ORISON SWETT MARDEN

Wealth stays with us a little moment if at all; only our characters are steadfast, not our gold.

EURIPIDES

Honesty

The glory that goes with wealth and beauty is fleeting and fragile; virtue is a possession glorious and eternal.

SALLUST

To measure the man measure his heart.

MALCOLM S. FORBES

Character before wealth.

AMOS LAWRENCE

Every germ of goodness will at last struggle into bloom and fruitage...true success follows every right step.

ORISON SWETT MARDEN

Work joyfully and peacefully, knowing that right thoughts and right efforts will inevitably bring about right results.

JAMES ALLEN

Honesty's the best policy.

MIGUEL DE CERVANTES, also
BENJAMIN FRANKLIN

And he shall be like a tree planted by the rivers of water, that bringeth forth his fruit in his season; his leaf also shall not wither; and whatsoever he doeth shall prosper.

Bible, PSALMS 1:3

Seeing all the possibilities,

seeing all that can be done,

and **how** it can be done,

marks the power of imagina-

tion. Our imagination is our

own personal laboratory. Here

Imagination

we can recreate events, map

out plans, and visualize over-

coming obstacles. Imagination

shows us how to turn

possibility into reality.

The will to do springs from the knowledge that we can do.

JAMES ALLEN

You must first clearly see a thing in your mind before you can do it.

ALEX MORRISON

The mind must see visual achievement of the purpose before action is initiated.

MACK R. DOUGLAS

Image creates desire. You will what you imagine.

J. G. GALLIMORE

Capability means imagination....

NAPOLEON HILL

Visualize this thing that you want. See it, feel it, believe in it. Make your mental blue print, and begin to build!

ROBERT COLLIER

For imagination sets the goal "picture" which our automatic mechanism works on. We act, or fail to act, not because of "will," as is so commonly believed, but because of imagination.

MAXWELL MALTZ

When the imagination and willpower are in conflict, are antagonistic, it is always the imagination which wins, without any exception.

EMILE COUÉ

hat you see is what you get.

FLIP WILSON

The imagination equips us to perceive reality when it is not fully materialized.

MARY CAROLINE RICHARDS

The source and center of all man's creative power... is his power of making images, or the power of imagination.

ROBERT COLLIER

Pictures help you to form the mental mold....

ROBERT COLLIER

When you think something, you think in pictures. You don't think a thought in words. You think a picture that expresses your thought. Working with this picture will produce it into your experience.

GRACE SPEARE

 man is not idle because he is absorbed in thought. There is a visible labour and there is an invisible labour.

VICTOR HUGO

My thoughts are my company; I can bring them together, select them, detain them, dismiss them.

WALTER SAVAGE LANDOR

hought makes every thing fit for use.

RALPH WALDO EMERSON

Imagination

First comes thought; then organization of that thought into ideas and plans; then transformation of those plans into reality. The beginning, as you will observe, is in your imagination.

NAPOLEON HILL

First have being in your mind. Make real in your mind then bring that being into reality....The genius is he who sees what is not yet and causes it to come to be.

PETER NIVIO ZARLENGA

The great successful men of the world have used their imaginations...they think ahead and create their mental picture, and then go to work materializing that picture in all its details, filling in here, adding a little there, altering this a bit and that a bit, but steadily building—steadily building.

ROBERT COLLIER

Study the situation thoroughly, go over in your imagination the various courses of action possible to you and the consequences which can and may follow from each course. Pick out the course which gives the most promise—and go ahead.

MAXWELL MALTZ

Make every thought, every fact, that comes into your mind pay you a profit. Make it work and produce for you. Think of things not as they are but as they might be....Don't merely dream—but create!

ROBERT COLLIER

Begin to imagine what the desirable outcome would be like. Go over these mental pictures and delineate details and refinements. Play them over and over to yourself.

MAXWELL MALTZ

We are told never to cross a bridge till we come to it, but this world is owned by men who have "crossed bridges" in their imagination far ahead of the crowd.

SPEAKERS LIBRARY

The entrepreneur is essentially a visualizer and an actualizer....He can visualize something, and when he visualizes it he sees exactly how to make it happen.

ROBERT L. SCHWARTZ

Try out your ideas by visualizing them in action.

DAVID SEABURY

Mentally imagine you are buying the business or applying for the job that will earn your fortune. Review each step you'd take, the obstacles you might meet, the difficulties you would meet. Continue imagining each step until you mentally reach your wealth goal.

TYLER G. HICKS

A man to carry on a successful business must have imagination. He must see things in a vision, a dream of the whole thing.

CHARLES M. SCHWAB

Developing a prototype early is the number one goal for our designers, or anyone else who has an idea, for that matter. We don't trust it until we can see it and feel it.

WIN NG

My method is different. I do not rush into actual work. When I get a new idea, I start at once building it up in my imagination, and make improvements and operate the device in my mind....When I have gone so far as to embody everything in my invention, every possible improvement I can think of, and when I see no fault anywhere, I put into concrete form the final product of my brain.

NIKOLA TESLA

Imagination

The real trick is to make the moves in your head first, as a way of testing them out.

JULIENE BERK

By going over your day in imagination before you begin it, you can begin acting successfully at any moment.

DOROTHEA BRANDE

Imagination....Its limits are only those of the mind itself.

ROD SERLING

Ideas cross mountains, borders, and seas. They go anywhere a man can go....

The HOUSTON TIMES

Surely there is grandeur in knowing that in the realm of thought, at least, you are without a chain; that you have the right to explore all heights and all depths; that there are no walls nor fences, nor prohibited places, nor sacred corners in all the vast expanse of thought....

ROBERT G. INGERSOLL

I am thought.
I can see what the eyes cannot see.
I can hear what the ears cannot hear.
I can feel what the heart cannot feel.

PETER NIVIO ZARLENGA

Nimble thought can jump both sea and land.

WILLIAM SHAKESPEARE

Thought is free.

WILLIAM SHAKESPEARE

Dreams are free.

UNKNOWN

"**T**o fly as fast as thought, to anywhere that is,"
He said, "You must begin by knowing that you have
already arrived."

RICHARD BACH, from
Jonathan Livingston Seagull

See the things you want as already yours....Think of
them as yours, as belonging to you, as already in
your possession.

ROBERT COLLIER

Picture yourself in your minds eye as having already
achieved this goal. See yourself doing the things
you'll be doing when you've reached your goal.

EARL NIGHTINGALE

I noticed an almost universal trait among Super
Achievers, and it was what I call Sensory Goal Vision.
These people knew what they wanted out of life, and they
could sense it multidimensionally before they ever had it.
They could not only see it, but also taste it, smell it, and
imagine the sounds and emotions associated with it. They
pre-lived it before they had it. And that sharp, sensory
vision became a powerful driving force in their lives.

STEVEN DeVORE

I've discovered that numerous peak performers use
the skill of mental rehearsal or visualization....They
mentally run through important events before they happen.

CHARLES A. GARFIELD

I visualize things in my mind before I have to do
them....It's like having a mental workshop.

JACK YOUNGBLOOD

Imagination

The imagination is literally the workshop wherein are fashioned all plans created by man.

NAPOLEON HILL

By visualizing your goals, you can get your subconscious to work toward making these mental pictures come true.

SUCCESS MAGAZINE

See things as you would have them be instead of as they are.

ROBERT COLLIER

We have been endowed with the capacity and the power to create desirable pictures within and to find them automatically printed in the outer world of our environment.

JOHN McDONALD

We can gradually grow into any conditions we desire, provided we first make ourselves in habitual mental attitude the person who corresponds to those conditions....

THOMAS TROWARD

Picture yourself vividly as winning, and that alone will contribute immeasurably to success.

HARRY EMERSON FOSDICK

The courage to begin separates

dreamers from achievers.

Starting is the key: because

if we want to be successful,

we must start sometime.

The willingness to act—to

overcome inertia—is the first

step on the path to greatness.

Inertia

The first step is the hardest.

MARIE DE VICHY-CHAMROND

Every body continues in its state of rest, or of uniform motion in a right line, unless it is compelled to change that state by forces impressed upon it.

SIR ISAAC NEWTON

The natural law of inertia: Matter will remain at rest or continue in uniform motion in the same straight line unless acted upon by some external force.

W. CLEMENT STONE

That's why many fail—because they don't get started—they don't go. They don't overcome inertia. They don't begin.

W. CLEMENT STONE

The fool with all his other thoughts, has this also: he is always getting ready to live.

EPICURUS

We are always getting ready to live, but never living.

RALPH WALDO EMERSON

There are those of us who are always about to live. We are waiting until things change, until there is more time, until we are less tired, until we get a promotion, until we settle down—until, until, until. It always seems as if there is some major event that must occur in our lives before we begin living.

GEORGE SHEEHAN

To be always intending to live a new life, but never find time to set about it—this is as if a man should put off eating and drinking from one day to another till he be starved and destroyed.

SIR WALTER SCOTT

The worst thing one can do is not to try, to be aware of what one wants and not give in to it, to spend years in silent hurt wondering if something could have materialized—and never knowing.

DAVID VISCOTT

For of all sad words of tongue or pen, the saddest are these: "It might have been!"

JOHN GREENLEAF WHITTIER

We will not know unless we begin.

HOWARD ZINN

Your difficulty and my difficulty and the difficulty of every individual who ever desired to achieve something worthwhile, comes in the movement.

PETER NIVIO ZARLENGA

Taking a new step, uttering a new word, is what people fear most.

FYODOR DOSTOEVSKY

The greatest of all mistakes is to do nothing because you can only do a little. Do what you can.

SYDNEY SMITH

Nothing will ever be attempted if all possible objections must first be overcome.

SAMUEL JOHNSON

Inertia

If you could get up the courage to begin, you have the courage to succeed.

DAVID VISCOTT

Once you're moving you can keep moving.

RONALD ALAN WEISS

The common conception is that motivation leads to action, but the reverse is true—action precedes motivation. You have to "prime the pump" and get the juices flowing, which motivates you to work on your goals. Getting momentum going is the most difficult part of the job, and often taking the first step...is enough to prompt you to make the best of your day.

ROBERT J. McKAIN

The only true failure lies in failure to start.

HAROLD BLAKE WALKER

Are you in earnest? Seize this very minute! Boldness has genius, power, and magic in it. Only engage, and then the mind grows heated. Begin, and then the work will be completed.

JOHN ANSTER, Faust, Prologue for the Theatre, manager's speech

It's the job that's never started as takes longest to finish.

J. R. R. TOLKIEN

A good beginning cometh a good end.

JOHN HEYWOOD

A work well begun is half ended.

PLATO

Well begun is half done.

ARISTOTLE

He who has begun has half done.

HORACE

Eighty percent of success is showing up.

WOODY ALLEN

Begin to free yourself at once by doing all that is possible with the means you have, and as you proceed in this spirit the way will open for you to do more.

ROBERT COLLIER

It is the direction and not the magnitude which is to be taken into consideration.

THOMAS TROWARD

Our grand business is not to see what lies dimly at a distance, but to do what lies clearly at hand.

THOMAS CARLYLE

When we are sure that we are on the right road there is no need to plan our journey too far ahead; no need to burden ourselves with doubts and fears as to the obstacles that may bar our progress. We cannot take more than one step at a time.

ORISON SWETT MARDEN

The difficulties you meet will resolve themselves as you advance. Proceed, and light will dawn, and shine with increasing clearness on your path.

D'ALEMBERT

Inertia

To solve a problem or to reach a goal, you...don't need to know all the answers in advance. But you must have a clear idea of the problem or the goal you want to reach.

W. CLEMENT STONE

All you have to do is know where you're going. The answers will come to you of their own accord.

EARL NIGHTINGALE

Everyone who achieves success in a great venture, solved each problem as they came to it. They helped themselves. And they were helped through powers known and unknown to them at the time they set out on their voyage. They kept going regardless of the obstacles they met.

W. CLEMENT STONE

If you procrastinate when faced with a big difficult problem...break the problem into parts, and handle one part at a time.

ROBERT COLLIER

Have a bias toward action—let's see something happen now. You can break that big plan into small steps and take the first step right away.

RICHARD THALHEIMER

Winning starts with beginning.

ROBERT H. SCHULLER

Some people, in working toward a goal, find themselves seized by inertia when it comes time for action. If this should happen to you, despite the small graduated steps, then it is time to reexamine your goal. Consider how important it actually is and then either discard the goal (and replace it with a more suitable one) or continue the steps with a renewed sense of the value of achieving it.

FITZHUGH DODSON

Love is the most important
ingredient of success. Without
it, our life echoes emptiness.

With it, our life vibrates
warmth and meaning. Even in
hardship, love shines through.
Therefore, search for love. Once
we have learned to love, we
will have learned to live.

I argue thee that love is life
And life hath immortality.

EMILY DICKINSON

Love is something eternal.

VINCENT VAN GOGH

The cure for all the ills and wrongs, the cares, the sorrows, and the crimes of humanity, all lie in that one word "love." It is the divine vitality that everywhere produces and restores life.

LYDIA MARIA CHILD

Life in abundance comes only through great love.

ELBERT HUBBARD

We are all born for love. It is the principle of existence, and its only end.

BENJAMIN DISRAELI

Is it not by love alone that we succeed in penetrating to the very essence of a being?

IGOR STRAVINSKY

Love is the immortal flow of energy that nourishes, extends and preserves. Its eternal goal is life.

SMILEY BLANTON

Love is the emblem of eternity: it confounds all notion of time: effaces all memory of a beginning, all fear of an end.

ANNA LOUISE DE STAËL

Human love....It is that extra creation that stands hurt and baffled at the place of death....Being human, wanting children and sunlight and breath to go on, forever.

CHRISTOPHER LEACH

What force is more potent than love?

IGOR STRAVINSKY

We live in the world when we love it.

RABINDRANATH TAGORE

Take away love and our earth is a tomb.

ROBERT BROWNING

A place is nothing, not even space, unless at its heart a figure stands.

AMY LOWELL

The way is not in the sky
The way is in the heart.

GAUTAMA BUDDHA

To fail to love is not to exist at all.

MARK VAN DOREN

Love is the river of life in this world.

HENRY WARD BEECHER

If you have it, you don't need to have anything else, and if you don't have it, it doesn't much matter what else you have.

SIR JAMES M. BARRIE

Love is all you need.

JOHN LENNON and
PAUL McCARTNEY

Love is the only gold.

ALFRED LORD TENNYSON

Love is all we have.

EURIPIDES

Love is everything. It is the key to life, and its influences are those that move the world.

RALPH WALDO TRINE

No thoughtful man ever came to the end of his life, and had time and a little space of calm from which to look back upon it, who did not know and acknowledge that it was what he had done unselfishly and for others, and nothing else, that satisfied him in the retrospect, and made him feel that he had played the man.

WOODROW WILSON

The best portion of a good man's life,—his little nameless, unremembered acts of kindness and of love.

WILLIAM WORDSWORTH

You will find as you look back upon your life that the moments that stand out, the moments when you have really lived, are the moments when you have done things in a spirit of love.

HENRY DRUMMOND

Do all things with love.

OG MANDINO

The moment you have in your heart this extraordinary thing called love and feel the depth, the delight, the ecstacy of it, you will discover that for you the world is transformed.

J. KRISHNAMURTI

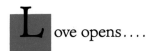**L**ove opens....

ROBERT COLLIER

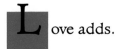**L**ove adds.

ROBERT COLLIER

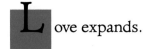**L**ove expands.

HUGH PRATHER

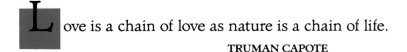**L**ove is a chain of love as nature is a chain of life.

TRUMAN CAPOTE

Love is the only bow on life's dark cloud. It is the Morning and Evening Star. It shines upon the cradle of the babe, and sheds its radiance upon the quiet tomb. It is the Mother of Art, inspirer of poet, patriot, and philosopher. It is the air and light of every heart, builder of every home, kindler of every fire on every hearth. It was the first dream of immortality. It fills the world with melody....Love is the magician, the enchanter, that changes worthless things to joy, and makes right royal kings of common clay.

ROBERT G. INGERSOLL

Love means the body, the soul, the life, the entire being. We feel love as we feel the warmth of our blood, we breathe love as we breathe the air, we hold it in ourselves as we hold our thoughts. Nothing more exists for us.

GUY DE MAUPASSANT

Love

Whether life is worth living depends on whether there is love in life.

R. D. LAING

Once you have learned to love,
You will have learned to live.

UNKNOWN

Treasure the love you receive above all. It will survive long after your gold and good health have vanished.

OG MANDINO

Where there is love there is life....

MOHANDAS GANDHI

Love is life....And if you miss love, you miss life.

LEO BUSCAGLIA

We know that we have passed from death into life, because we love....

Bible, I JOHN 3:14

There is a land of the living and a land of the dead and the bridge is love, the only survival, the only meaning.

THORNTON WILDER

To love abundantly is to live abundantly, and to love forever is to live forever.

HENRY DRUMMOND

On the last analysis, then, love is life. Love never faileth and life never faileth so long as there is love.

HENRY DRUMMOND

Goals are what keep us going. To be continually working is not enough. We must see clearly the next step. To keep moving after achieving one goal, we must set a new one.

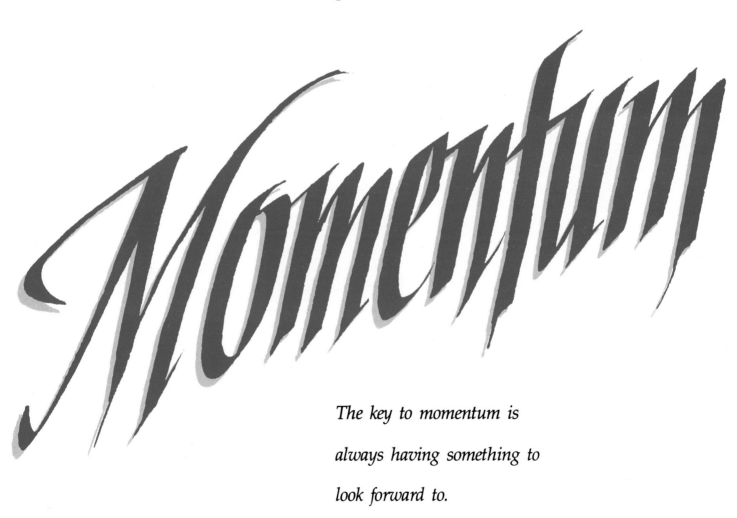

The key to momentum is always having something to look forward to.

Momentum

People who say that life is not worthwhile are really saying that they themselves have no personal goals which are worthwhile....Get yourself a goal worth working for. Better still, get yourself a project....Always have something ahead of you to "look forward to"—to work for and hope for.

MAXWELL MALTZ

One way to keep momentum going is to have constantly greater goals.

MICHAEL KORDA

What keeps me going is goals.

MUHAMMAD ALI

Man was created as a being who should constantly keep improving, a being who on reaching one goal sets a higher one.

RALPH RANSOM

What's important is that one strives to achieve a goal.

RONALD REAGAN

There must be a goal at every stage of life! There must be a goal!

MAGGIE KUHN

Always be planning something.

JOHN A. SCHINDLER

Give yourself something to work toward—constantly.

MARY KAY ASH

You have to erect a fence and say "OK, scale this."

LINDA RONSTADT

Money flows to an idea. And all riches begin in the mind. The starting point is to see what others want and to think of how to provide it. People will pay for a product or service they want. The idea will attract

*the money which follows. You **can** think and grow rich!*

Motivation

Everything is something I decide to do, and there is nothing I have to do.

DENIS E. WAITLEY

You don't have to do anything you don't want to do.

DAVID HAROLD FINK

Nobody *HAS* to do anything.

CHARLES McCABE

You can choose to be lazy or you can choose to be ambitious. Stop to think about it again. Don't you do your own choosing?

J. MARTIN KOHE

Decide that you really want to achieve the goal....

ROBERT J. McKAIN

We may think there is willpower involved, but more likely...change is due to want power. Wanting the new addiction more than the old one. Wanting the new me in preference to the...person I am now.

GEORGE SHEEHAN

You will suddenly realize that the reason you never changed before was because you didn't want to.

ROBERT H. SCHULLER

We do pretty much whatever we want to.

PHILLIP JOHNSON

It's so hard when I have to,
And so easy when I want to.

SONDRA ANICE BARNES

It....is not something I must do but something I want to do....

JAMES FIXX

We accomplish things by directing our desires, not by ignoring them.

UNKNOWN

How badly do you want it?

GEORGE ALLEN

Make sure you want it enough.

FRANK KINGDON

Inhabit ourselves that we may indeed do what we want to do.

MARY CAROLINE RICHARDS

Realize what you really want. It stops you from chasing butterflies and puts you to work digging gold.

WILLIAM MOULTON MARSTON

One of the reasons it has seemed so difficult for a person to change his habits, his personality, or his way of life, has been that heretofore nearly all efforts at change have been directed to the circumference of the self, so to speak, rather than to the center.

MAXWELL MALTZ

The inner thought coming from the heart represents the real motives and desires. These are the causes of action.

RAYMOND HOLLIWELL

Motivation

The most important thing about a man is what he believes in the depth of his being. This is the thing that makes him what he is, the thing that organizes him and feeds him; the thing that keeps him going in the face of untoward circumstances; the thing that gives him resistance and drive.

HUGH STEVENSON TIGNER

The key to every man is his thought. Sturdy and defying though he look, he has a helm which he obeys, which is the idea after which all his facts are classified. He can only be reformed by showing him a new idea which commands his own.

RALPH WALDO EMERSON

Everyone has his reasons.

JEAN RENOIR

You cannot teach a man anything. You can only help him to discover it within himself.

GALILEO GALILEI

The art of teaching is the art of assisting discovery.

MARK VAN DOREN

There is only one way...to get anybody to do anything....And that is by making the other person want to do it.

DALE CARNEGIE

To make men do what they want to do....

MAURICE BLONDEL

I have found the best way to give advice to your children is to find out what they want and then advise them to do it.

HARRY S. TRUMAN

Help people become more motivated by guiding them to the source of their own power.

PAUL G. THOMAS

People should follow their own energy.

WILL SCHULTZ

What is necessary to change a person is to change his awareness of himself.

ABRAHAM H. MASLOW

When a person acts without knowledge of what he thinks, feels, needs or wants, he does not yet have the option of choosing to act differently.

CLARK MOUSTAKAS

Self-observation brings man to the realization of the necessity of self-change. And in observing himself a man notices that self-observation itself brings about certain changes in his inner processes. He begins to understand that self-observation is an instrument of self-change, a means of awakening.

GEORGE GURDJIEFF

Face the fact of being what you are, for that is what changes what you are.

SÖREN KIERKEGAARD

Let us ask ourselves: "What kind of people do we think we are?"

RONALD REAGAN

Give the man you'd like to be a look at the man you are.

EDGAR A. GUEST

Motivation

Once a person says, "This is who I really am, what I am all about, what I was really meant to do," it is easier to decide how to spend one's time.

DAVID VISCOTT

Your desires and true beliefs have a way of playing blindman's bluff. You must corner the inner facts....

DAVID SEABURY

Whatever games are played with us, we must play no games with ourselves....

RALPH WALDO EMERSON

We lie loudest when we lie to ourselves.

ERIC HOFFER

Who has deceived thee so often as thyself?

BENJAMIN FRANKLIN

Take a look at your natural river. What are you? Stop playing games with yourself....Where's your river going? Are you riding with it? Or are you rowing against it?....Don't you see that there is no effort if you're riding with your river?

CARL FREDERICK

When we are not honest, we are cut off from a significant resource of ourselves, a vital dimension that is necessary for unity and wholeness.

CLARK MOUSTAKAS

Just be honest with yourself. That opens the door.

VERNON HOWARD

Successful people have cultivated the habit of never denying to themselves their true feelings and attitudes.... They have no need for pretenses.

DAVID HAROLD FINK

When you accept yourself completely you do not have to maintain a phony front, drive yourself to "achieve" or feel insecure if people tune-in to you and what you are doing.

KEN KEYES, JR.

Where is the man who has the strength to be true, and to show himself as he is?

JOHANN WOLFGANG VON GOETHE

Make sure you visualize what you really want, not what someone else wants for you.

JERRY GILLIES

We forfeit three-fourths of ourselves in order to be like other people.

ARTHUR SCHOPENHAUER

Am I motivated by what I really want out of life—or am I mass-motivated?

EARL NIGHTINGALE

No man, for any considerable period, can wear one face to himself, and another to the multitude, without finally getting bewildered as to which may be the true.

NATHANIEL HAWTHORNE

Motivation

Any person who recognizes this greatest power...the power to choose....Begins to realize that he is the one that is doing the choosing and that friends, although they mean well, cannot do his choosing for him, nor can his relatives. Consequently, he develops real self-confidence based upon his own ability, upon his own actions, and upon his own initiative.

J. MARTIN KOHE

You will live your life secure in that you are no longer manipulated by what other people want you to do and be, but are directed by your own inner desires.

H. STANLEY JUDD

If a man does not keep pace with his companions, perhaps it is because he hears a different drummer. Let him step to the music which he hears, however measured or far away.

HENRY DAVID THOREAU

If...I have lost every other friend on earth, I shall at least have one friend left, and that friend shall be down inside of me.

ABRAHAM LINCOLN

What we must try to be, of course, is ourselves...and wholeheartedly. We must find out what we really are and what we really want....

NELSON BOSWELL

You have to know what's important and what's unimportant, for you.

DAVID HAROLD FINK

Self knowers always dwell in El Dorado; they drink from the fountain of youth, and are at all times owners of all they wish to enjoy.

CLAUDE M. BRISTOL

In the middle of difficulty lies opportunity.

ALBERT EINSTEIN

Each problem has hidden in it an opportunity so powerful that it literally dwarfs the problem. The greatest success stories were created by people who recognized a problem and turned it into an opportunity.

JOSEPH SUGARMAN

As fast as each opportunity presents itself, use it! No matter how tiny an opportunity it may be, use it!

ROBERT COLLIER

Opportunities multiply as they are seized....

JOHN WICKER

What is luck? It is not only chance, it is also creating the opportunity, recognizing it when it is there, and taking it when it comes.

NATASHA JOSEFOWITZ

I think the harder you work, the more luck you have.

R. DAVID THOMAS

I'm a great believer in luck, and I find the harder I work the more I have of it.

THOMAS JEFFERSON

Things don't turn up in this world until somebody turns them up.

JAMES A. GARFIELD

Make the iron hot by striking it.

OLIVER CROMWELL

Opportunity

Destiny is not a matter of chance; it is a matter of choice. It is not something to be waited for; but, rather something to be achieved.

WILLIAM JENNINGS BRYAN

The best men are not those who have waited for chances but who have taken them; besieged the chance; conquered the chance; and made chance the servitor.

E. H. CHAPIN

Men who are resolved to find a way for themselves will always find opportunities enough; and if they do not lie ready to their hand, they will make them.

SAMUEL SMILES

Don't wait for extraordinary opportunities. Seize common occasions and make them great...weak men wait for opportunities; strong men make them.

ORISON SWETT MARDEN

The people who get on in this world are the people who get up and look for the circumstances they want, and, if they can't find them, make them.

GEORGE BERNARD SHAW

A wise man will make more opportunities than he finds.

FRANCIS BACON

You must make your own opportunities....

JOHN B. GOUGH

There will always be a frontier where there is an open mind and a willing hand.

CHARLES F. KETTERING

Peace comes when we live in a spirit of love. To get along with others, we must love them without forcing our love upon them. Imposing our beliefs

upon others will not bring peace. To have concern for others, to respect their rights and freedoms, and to let them be themselves—this is peace.

Peace

Do to others what you would have them do to you....

Bible, MATTHEW 7:12

What you do not wish others should do unto you, do not so unto them.

CONFUCIUS

Thou shalt love thy neighbor as thyself.

Bible, ROMANS 13:9

To love our neighbor as ourself is such a truth for regulating human society, that by that alone one might determine all the cases in social morality.

JOHN LOCKE

Consideration for others is the basis of a good life, a good society.

CONFUCIUS

The welfare of each is bound up in the welfare of all.

HELEN KELLER

Regard your neighbor's gain as your own gain, and your neighbor's loss as your own loss.

TAI SHANG KAN YING P'IEN

This is the sum of all—righteousness. In causing pleasure or in giving pain, in doing good or injury to others, a man obtains a proper rule of action by looking at his neighbor as himself.

THE MAHABHARATA

Harmony is one phase of the great law whose spiritual expression is love.

JAMES ALLEN

Adapt yourself to the things among which your lot has been cast and love sincerely the fellow creatures with whom destiny has ordained that you shall live.

MARCUS AURELIUS

To keep the Golden Rule we must put ourselves in other people's places, but to do that consists in and depends upon picturing ourselves in their places.

HARRY EMERSON FOSDICK

It is understanding that gives us an ability to have peace. When we understand the other fellow's viewpoint, and he understands ours, then we can sit down and work out our differences.

HARRY S. TRUMAN

Yes, we are all different. Different customs, different foods, different mannerisms, different languages, but not so different that we cannot get along with one another...if we will disagree without being disagreeable.

J. MARTIN KOHE

Let the ideas clash but not the hearts.

C. C. MEHTA

Who are enemies? Those who oppose each others will.

MARY CAROLINE RICHARDS

Selfishness is not living as one wishes to live; it is asking others to live as one wishes to live. And unselfishness is letting other people's lives alone, not interfering with them. Selfishness always aims at uniformity of type. Unselfishness recognizes infinite variety of type as a delightful thing, accepts it, acquiesces in it, enjoys it.

OSCAR WILDE

A wise unselfishness is not a surrender of yourself to the wishes of anyone, but only to the best discoverable course of action.

DAVID SEABURY

Live and let live.

JOHANN VON SCHILLER

Live and let live is the rule of common justice.

SIR ROGER L'ESTRANGE

The wise man....If he would live at peace with others, he will bear and forbear.

SAMUEL SMILES

If you want to get along, go along.

SAM RAYBURN

The love of liberty is the love of others; the love of power is the love of ourselves.

WILLIAM HAZLITT

We cannot force...love.

WILLIAM HAZLITT

Love....force it and it disappears. You cannot will love, nor even control it. You can only guide its expression. It comes or it goes according to those qualities in life that invite it or deny its presence.

DAVID SEABURY

Forcible ways make not an end of evil, but leave hatred and malice behind them.

SIR THOMAS BROWNE

Force is all-conquering, but its victories are short-lived.

ABRAHAM LINCOLN

We look forward to the time when the Power of Love will replace the Love of Power. Then will our world know the blessings of Peace.

WILLIAM EWART GLADSTONE

Hate can only flourish where love is absent.

WILLIAM C. MENNINGER

Men are not against you; they are merely for themselves.

GENE FOWLER

War grows out of the desire of the individual to gain advantage at the expense of his fellow men....

NAPOLEON HILL

Peace

We used to wonder where war lived, what it was that made it so vile. And now we realize that we know where it lives, that it is inside ourselves.

ALBERT CAMUS

There are weapons that are simply thoughts.... For the record, prejudices can kill and suspicion can destroy....

ROD SERLING

Wars begin in the minds of men, and in those minds, love and compassion would have built the defenses of peace.

U THANT

Hatred can be overcome only by love.

MOHANDAS GANDHI

Never in this world can hatred be stilled by hatred; it will be stilled only by non-hatred—this is the law eternal.

GAUTAMA BUDDHA

Love [is stronger] than violence.

HERMANN HESSE

The value of love will always be stronger than the value of hate.... Any nation or group of nations which employs hatred eventually is torn to pieces by hatred....

FRANKLIN DELANO ROOSEVELT

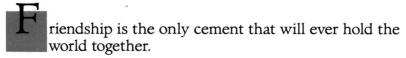riendship is the only cement that will ever hold the world together.

WOODROW WILSON

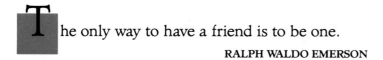he only way to have a friend is to be one.

RALPH WALDO EMERSON

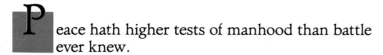et us ever remember that our interest is in concord, not in conflict; and that our real eminence rests in the victories of peace, not those of war.

WILLIAM McKINLEY

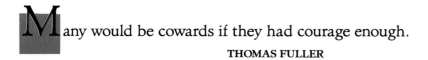eace hath higher tests of manhood than battle ever knew.

JOHN GREENLEAF WHITTIER

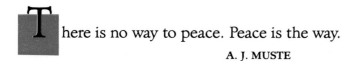any would be cowards if they had courage enough.

THOMAS FULLER

The place to improve the world is first in one's own heart and head and hands....

ROBERT M. PIRSIG

There is no way to peace. Peace is the way.

A. J. MUSTE

When the wish for peace is genuine, the means for finding it is given in a form each mind that seeks for it in honesty can understand.

HELEN SCHUCMAN and
WILLIAM THETFORD

Peace

If we have no peace, it is because we have forgotten that we belong to each other.

MOTHER TERESA

By this all men will know that you are my disciples, if you have love for one another.

Bible, JOHN 13:35

For one human being to love another: that is perhaps the most difficult of all our tasks, the ultimate, the last test and proof, the work for which all other work is but preparation.

RAINER MARIA RILKE

The power to hold on in spite
of everything, to endure—this is
the winner's quality. Persistence
is the ability to face defeat

Persistence

again and again without giving
up—to push on in the face of
great difficulty. Persistence
means taking pains to overcome
every obstacle, to do all that's
necessary to reach our goals.

Persistence

Success...seems to be connected with action. Successful men keep moving. They make mistakes, but they don't quit.

CONRAD HILTON

If I had to select one quality, one personal characteristic that I regard as being most highly correlated with success, whatever the field, I would pick the trait of persistence. Determination. The will to endure to the end, to get knocked down seventy times and get up off the floor saying, "Here goes number seventy-one!"

RICHARD M. DeVOS

I do not think there is any other quality so essential to success of any kind as the quality of perseverance. It overcomes almost everything, even nature.

JOHN D. ROCKEFELLER

Success seems to be largely a matter of hanging on after others have let go.

WILLIAM FEATHER

History has demonstrated that the most notable winners usually encountered heartbreaking obstacles before they triumphed. They won because they refused to become discouraged by their defeats.

B. C. FORBES

Endurance is the crowning quality....

JAMES RUSSELL LOWELL

Nothing in the world can take the place of persistence. Talent will not; nothing is more common than unsuccessful men with talent. Genius will not; unrewarded genius is almost a proverb. Education will not; the world is full of educated derelicts. Persistence and determination alone are omnipotent.

CALVIN COOLIDGE

Every great work, every big accomplishment, has been brought into manifestation through holding to the vision, and often just before the big achievement, comes apparent failure and discouragement.

FLORENCE SCOVEL SHINN

Before success comes in any man's life he is sure to meet with much temporary defeat and, perhaps, some failure. When defeat overtakes a man, the easiest and most logical thing to do is to quit. That is exactly what the majority of men do.

NAPOLEON HILL

Never give up then, for that is just the place and time that the tide will turn.

HARRIET BEECHER STOW

What we do not see, what most of us never suspect of existing, is the silent but irresistible power which comes to the rescue of those who fight on in the face of discouragement.

NAPOLEON HILL

What this power is I cannot say; all I know is that it exists and it becomes available only when a man is in that state of mind in which he knows exactly what he wants and is fully determined not to quit until he finds it.

ALEXANDER GRAHAM BELL

Effort only fully releases its reward after a person refuses to quit.

NAPOLEON HILL

How many a man has thrown up his hands at a time when a little more effort, a little more patience, would have achieved success?

ELBERT HUBBARD

Persistence

Nearly every man who develops an idea works it up to the point where it looks impossible, and then gets discouraged. That's not the place to become discouraged.

THOMAS A. EDISON

Most people give up just when they're about to achieve success. They quit on the one yard line. They give up at the last minute of the game, one foot from a winning touchdown.

H. ROSS PEROT

Some men give up their designs when they have almost reached the goal; while others, on the contrary, obtain a victory by exerting, at the last moment, more vigorous efforts than ever before.

HERODOTUS

You just keep pushing. You just keep pushing. I made every mistake that could be made. But I just kept pushing.

RENE McPHERSON

When I have fully decided that a result is worth getting I go ahead on it and make trial after trial until it comes.

THOMAS A. EDISON

The miracle, or the power, that elevates the few is to be found in their industry, application, and perseverance under the promptings of a brave, determined spirit.

MARK TWAIN

Austere perseverance, harsh and continuous...rarely fails of its purpose, for its silent power grows irresistibly greater with time.

JOHANN WOLFGANG VON GOETHE

All great achievements require time.

DAVID JOSEPH SCHWARTZ

Perpetual pushing and assurance put a difficulty out of countenance and make a seeming difficulty give way.

JEREMY COLLIER

It's the constant and determined effort that breaks down all resistance, sweeps away all obstacles.

CLAUDE M. BRISTOL

Few things are impossible to diligence and skill.... Great works are performed not by strength, but perseverance.

SAMUEL JOHNSON

Life is queer with its twists and turns,
As everyone of us sometime learns,
And many a failure turns about,
When he might have won had he stuck it out,
Don't give up though the race seems slow,
You may succeed with another blow.

Success is failure turned inside out,
The silver tint of the clouds of doubt,
And you never can tell how close you are,
It may be near when it seems so far.
So stick to the fight when you're hardest hit,
It's when things seem worse,
That you must not quit.

UNKNOWN

If at first you don't succeed, try, try, try again.

WILLIAM E. HICKSON

When you get right down to the root of the meaning of the word "succeed," you find that it simply means to follow through.

F. W. NICHOL

Persistence

Try, try, try, and keep trying is the rule that must be followed to become an expert in anything.

W. CLEMENT STONE

Never, never, never, never give up.

WINSTON CHURCHILL

If you only knock long enough and loud enough at the gate, you are sure to wake up somebody.

HENRY WADSWORTH LONGFELLOW

You may have a fresh start any moment you choose, for this thing that we call "failure" is not the falling down, but the staying down.

MARY PICKFORD

Our greatest glory is not in never falling, but in rising every time we fall.

CONFUCIUS

It's not whether you get knocked down. It's whether you get up again.

VINCE LOMBARDI

You become a champion by fighting one more round. When things are tough, you fight one more round.

JAMES J. CORBETT

It's not over until it's over.

YOGI BERRA

If you've got the guts to stick it out...you're going to make it.

BRIAN HAYS

He conquers who endures.

PERSIUS

To be vanquished and yet not surrender, that is victory.

JOSEF PILSUDSKI

Plodding wins the race.

AESOP

Those who commence deliberately. They plod on. They stick to it....They persevere and finally reap their reward.

CHARLES E. POPPLESTONE

It is not necessary to hope in order to undertake, nor to succeed in order to persevere.

CHARLES THE BOLD

In each age men of genius undertake the ascent. From below, the world follows them with their eyes. These men go up the mountain, enter the clouds, disappear, reappear. People watch them, mark them. They walk by the side of precipices. They daringly pursue their road. See them aloft, see them in the distance; they are but black specks. On they go. The road is uneven, its difficulties constant. At each step a wall, at each step a trap. As they rise the cold increases. They must make their ladder, cut the ice and walk on it, hewing the steps in haste. A storm is raging. Nevertheless they go forward in their madness. The air becomes difficult to breathe. The abyss yawns below them. Some fall. Others stop and retrace their steps; there is a sad weariness.

The bold ones continue. They are eyed by the eagles; the lightning plays about them; the hurricane is furious. No matter, they persevere.

VICTOR HUGO

Persistence

It takes a little courage
And a little self-control
And some grim determination,
If you want to reach the goal.

It takes a deal of striving,
And a firm and stern-set chin,
No matter what the battle,
If you really want to win.

There's no easy path to glory,
There's no rosy road to fame.
Life, however we may view it,
Is no simple parlor game;

But its prizes call for fighting,
For endurance and for grit;
For a rugged disposition
And a don't-know-when-to-quit.

UNKNOWN

The majority of men meet with failure because of their lack of persistence in creating new plans to take the place of those which fail.

NAPOLEON HILL

In the end, the only people who fail are those who do not try.

DAVID VISCOTT

There is no failure except in no longer trying. There is no defeat except from within, no really insurmountable barrier save our own inherent weakness of purpose.

ELBERT HUBBARD

The odds are with us if we keep on trying.

KEITH DeGREEN

There's only one way you can fail—and that's to quit.

BRIAN HAYS

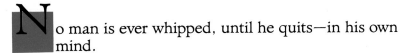

o man is ever whipped, until he quits—in his own mind.

NAPOLEON HILL

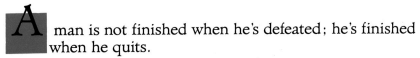

man is not finished when he's defeated; he's finished when he quits.

RICHARD M. NIXON

It is inevitable that some defeat will enter even the most victorious life. The human spirit is never finished when it is defeated...it is finished when it surrenders.

BEN STEIN

The rewards for those who persevere far exceed the pain that must precede the victory.

TED W. ENGSTROM and
R. ALEC MacKENZIE

Continuous, unflagging effort, persistence and determination will win. Let not the man be discouraged who has these.

JAMES WHITCOMB RILEY

Winning isn't everything, but wanting to win is.

VINCE LOMBARDI

The most essential factor is persistence,—the determination never to allow your energy or enthusiasm to be dampened by the discouragement that must inevitably come.

JAMES WHITCOMB RILEY

To have striven, to have made the effort, to have been true to certain ideals—this alone is worth the struggle.

WILLIAM OSLER

Persistence

If you can wait and not be tired by waiting....

RUDYARD KIPLING

If you can force your heart and nerve and sinew
To serve your turn long after they are gone,
And so hold on when there is nothing in you
Except the Will which says to them: "Hold on!"

RUDYARD KIPLING

It helps, I think, to consider ourselves on a very long journey: the main thing is to keep to the faith, to endure, to help each other when we stumble or tire, to weep and press on.

MARY CAROLINE RICHARDS

To endure is greater than to dare; to tire out hostile fortune; to be daunted by no difficulty; to keep heart when all have lost it; to go through intrigue spotless; to forego even ambition when the end is gained—who can say this is not greatness?

WILLIAM MAKEPEACE THACKERAY

I know of no such unquestionable badge and ensign of a sovereign mind as that of tenacity of purpose....

RALPH WALDO EMERSON

No, there is no failure for the man who realizes his power, who never knows when he is beaten; there is no failure for the determined endeavor; the unconquerable will. There is no failure for the man who gets up every time he falls, who rebounds like a rubber ball, who persists when every one else gives up, who pushes on when everyone else turns back.

ORISON SWETT MARDEN

Planning is like a road map. It can show us the way, head us in the right direction, and keep us on course. Planning means mapping out how to get from where we are now to where we

want to be. Planning is the power tool for achievement— the magic bridge to our goal.

Planning

It isn't sufficient just to want—you've got to ask yourself what you are going to do to get the things you want.

RICHARD ROSE

Your problem is to bridge the gap which exists between where you are now and the goal you intend to reach.

EARL NIGHTINGALE

How can we get from here to wherever it is we want to be?

NATASHA JOSEFOWITZ

The task of the leader is to get his people from where they are to where they have not been.

HENRY KISSINGER

The wise man bridges the gap by laying out the path by means of which he can get from where he is to where he wants to go.

JOHN J. B. MORGAN and EWING T. WEBB

I never did anything by accident, nor did any of my inventions come indirectly through accident....

THOMAS A. EDISON

At all times it is better to have a method.

MARK CAINE

With a definite, step-by-step plan—ah, what a difference it makes! You cannot fail, because each step carries you along to the next, like a track....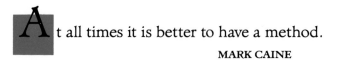

SCOTT REED

o one was ever lost on a straight road.

Proverb from INDIA

othing is likelier to keep a man within compass than having constantly before his eyes the state of his affairs in a regular course of account.

JOHN LOCKE

 good plan is like a road map: it shows the final destination and usually marks the best way to get there....

H. STANLEY JUDD

ll you need is the plan, the road map, and the courage to press on to your destination.

EARL NIGHTINGALE

omewhere there is a map of how it can be done.

BEN STEIN

very well built house started in the form of a definite purpose plus a definite plan in the nature of a set of blueprints.

NAPOLEON HILL

uccess or failure is often determined on the drawing board.

ROBERT J. McKAIN

lanning is bringing the future into the present so that you can do something about it now.

ALAN LAKEIN

Planning

Each man should frame life so that at some future hour fact and his dreamings meet.

VICTOR HUGO

When schemes are laid in advance, it is surprising how often the circumstances will fit in with them.

WILLIAM OSLER

The structure...will automatically provide the pattern for the action which follows.

DONALD CURTIS

Make your mold. The best flux in the world will not make a usable shape unless you have a mold to pour it in.

ROBERT COLLIER

Thoroughness characterizes all successful men. Genius is the art of taking infinite pains....All great achievement has been characterized by extreme care, infinite painstaking, even to the minutest detail.

ELBERT HUBBARD

Meticulous planning will enable everything a man does to appear spontaneous.

MARK CAINE

A good system shortens the road to the goal....

ORISON SWETT MARDEN

Whatever failures I have known, whatever errors I have committed, whatever follies I have witnessed in private and public life have been the consequence of action without thought.

BERNARD M. BARUCH

Our goals can only be reached through a vehicle of a plan, in which we must fervently believe, and upon which we must vigorously act. There is no other route to success.

STEPHEN A. BRENNEN

An intelligent plan is the first step to success. The man who plans knows where is is going, knows what progress he is making and has a pretty good idea when he will arrive.

BASIL S. WALSH

Strategic planning will help you fully uncover your available options, set priorities for them, and define the methods to achieve them.

ROBERT J. McKAIN

The best business plans are straightforward documents that spell out the "who, what, where, why, and how much...."

PAULA NELSON

What do you want to achieve or avoid? The answers to this question are your objectives.

How will you go about achieving your desired results? The answer to this you can call strategy.

WILLIAM E. ROTHSCHILD

Some self-confronting questions:
"Where do I want to be at any given time?"
"How am I going to get there?"
"What do I have to do to get myself from where I am to where I want to be?"....
"What's the first, small step I can take to get moving?"

GEORGE A. FORD and
GORDON L. LIPPITT

Planning

eveloping the plan is actually laying out the sequence of events that have to occur for you to achieve your goal.

GEORGE L. MORRISEY

A plan is a list of actions arranged in whatever sequence is thought likely to achieve an objective.

JOHN ARGENTI

Reduce your plan to writing.... The moment you complete this, you will have definitely given concrete form to the intangible desire.

NAPOLEON HILL

First you write down your goal; your second job is to break down your goal into a series of steps, beginning with steps which are absurdly easy.

FITZHUGH DODSON

Divide your movement into easy-to-do sections. If you fail, divide again.

PETER NIVIO ZARLENGA

The short-term plan, then, is an operative plan defining goals in writing and clearly indicating how these goals are to be carried out....

AMERICAN MANAGEMENT
ASSOCIATION

If you employed study, thinking, and planning time daily, you could develop and use the power that can change the course of your destiny.

W. CLEMENT STONE

Can you think of anything more permanently elating than to know that you are on the right road at last?

VERNON HOWARD

There are no limits to our

possibilities. At any moment,

we have more possibilities

than we can act upon. When

we imagine the possibilities,

our

vision expands, we capture

our dreams, and our life is

full. We can reach out and

touch the limits of our being.

Possibilities

There is far more opportunity than there is ability.

THOMAS A. EDISON

We have more than we use.

RALPH WALDO EMERSON

No matter what the level of your ability, you have more potential than you can ever develop in a lifetime.

JAMES T. McCAY

Your range of available choices—right now—is limitless.

CARL FREDERICK

The journey is difficult, immense.... We will travel as far as we can, but we cannot in one lifetime see all that we would like to see or to learn all that we hunger to know.

LOREN EISELEY

Few men during their lifetime come anywhere near exhausting the resources dwelling within them. There are deep wells of strength that are never used.

RICHARD E. BYRD

Deep within man dwell those slumbering powers; powers that would astonish him, that he never dreamed of possessing; forces that would revolutionize his life if aroused and put into action.

ORISON SWETT MARDEN

Compared to what we ought to be, we are only half awake. We are making use of only a small part of our physical and mental resources. Stating the thing broadly, the human individual thus lives far within his limits. He possesses power of various sorts which he habitually fails to use.

WILLIAM JAMES

There are powers inside of you which, if you could discover and use, would make of you everything you ever dreamed or imagined you could become.

ORISON SWETT MARDEN

We all have possibilities we don't know about. We can do things we don't even dream we can do.

DALE CARNEGIE

There is a great treasure there behind our skull and this is true about all of us. This little treasure has great, great powers, and I would say we only have learned a very, very small part of what it can do.

ISAAC BASHEVIS SINGER

You have powers you never dreamed of. You can do things you never thought you could do. There are no limitations in what you can do except the limitations of your own mind....

DARWIN P. KINGSLEY

Our thoughts and imaginations are the only real limits to our possibilities.

ORISON SWETT MARDEN, also
RALPH WALDO TRINE

The only lack or limitation is in your own mind.

N. H. MOOS

Every one's got it in him, if he'll only make up his mind and stick at it. None of us is born with a stop-valve on his powers or with a set limit to his capacities. There's no limit possible to the expansion of each one of us.

CHARLES M. SCHWAB

Possibilities

The barriers are not erected which can say to aspiring talents and industry, "Thus far and no farther."

LUDWIG VAN BEETHOVEN

If we all did the things we are capable of doing, we would literally astound ourselves.

THOMAS A. EDISON

The human spirit is so great a thing that no man can express it; could we rightly comprehend the mind of man nothing would be impossible to us upon the earth.

PARACELSUS

When the impossible has been eliminated, whatever remains, no matter how improbable...is possible.

SIR ARTHUR CONAN DOYLE

Everyone has inside of him a piece of good news. The good news is that you don't know how great you can be! How much you can love! What you can accomplish! And what your potential is!

ANNE FRANK

Within you right now is the power to do things you never dreamed possible. This power becomes available to you just as soon as you can change your beliefs.

MAXWELL MALTZ

We know what we are, but know not what we may be.

WILLIAM SHAKESPEARE

Look at things...as they can be.

DAVID JOSEPH SCHWARTZ

The power which resides in man is new in nature, and none but he knows what that is which he can do, nor does he know until he has tried.

RALPH WALDO EMERSON

No one knows what he can do till he tries.

PUBLILIUS SYRUS

Perhaps nobody ever accomplishes all that he feels lies in him to do; but nearly every one who tries his powers touches the walls of his being.

CHARLES DUDLEY WARNER

The richness of life, the love and joy and exhilaration of life can be found only with an upward look. This is an exciting world. It is cram-packed with opportunity. Great moments wait around every corner.

RICHARD M. DeVOS

Oh who can tell the range of joy or set the bounds of beauty?

SARA TEASDALE

To be alive—is power—
Existence—in itself—
Without a further function—
Omnipotence—enough—

EMILY DICKINSON

Better a thousand times even a swiftly fading, ephemeral moment of life than the epoch-long unconsciousness of the stone.

EDWIN WAY TEALE

Be glad of life because it gives you the chance....

HENRY VAN DYKE

Possibilities

While there's life, there's hope.

MARCUS TULLIUS CICERO

Every year I live I am more convinced that the waste of life lies in the love we have not given, the powers we have not used....

MARY CHOLMONDELEY

No one ever yet was the poorer in the long run for having once in a lifetime "let out all the length of all the reins."

MARY CHOLMONDELEY

The failure wishes he could do things he could never do. He thinks little of what he can do.

MARK CAINE

Everyone has a fair turn to be as great as he pleases.

JEREMY COLLIER

You can do anything you wish to do, have anything you wish to have, be anything you wish to be.

ROBERT COLLIER

Never say never.

ELIA KAZAN, also
ROBERT H. SCHULLER

There is no such thing as no chance.

HENRY FORD

There is always room at the top.

DANIEL WEBSTER

Power comes from knowing

how to do something. People

with power are people who

know how to get things

done. And sometimes knowing

how to do something is

virtually the same as having

done it. So when we educate

ourselves, we build power to

accomplish our goals.

Power

Power flows to the man who knows how.

ELBERT HUBBARD

Power gravitates to the man who knows how.

ORISON SWETT MARDEN

The king is the man who can.

THOMAS CARLYLE

Knowledge is more than equivalent to force.

SAMUEL JOHNSON

Knowledge itself is power.

FRANCIS BACON

Knowledge is power.

THOMAS HOBBES

Ideas....They have the power....

NAPOLEON HILL

Ideas are, in truth, forces.

HENRY JAMES

Thoughts are forces.

RALPH WALDO TRINE

Every thought you entertain is a force that goes out, and every thought comes back laden with its kind.

RALPH WALDO TRINE

There is no thought in any mind, but it quickly tends to convert itself into a power.

RALPH WALDO EMERSON

Every addition to true knowledge is an addition to human power....

HORACE MANN

Power is the by-product of understanding.

JACOB BRONOWSKI

Understanding brings control.

BONEWITZ

What we do not understand, we cannot control.

CHARLES REICH

To know is to control.

SCOTT REED

To know the right means of getting something done is virtually to have done it.

MARK CAINE

Our power is not so much in us as through us.

HARRY EMERSON FOSDICK

Knowledge comes by eyes always open and working hands; and there is no knowledge that is not power.

RALPH WALDO EMERSON

As a general rule the most successful man in life is the man who has the best information.

BENJAMIN DISRAELI

Power

The secret of business is to know something that nobody else knows.

ARISTOTLE ONASSIS

To succeed in a business, to reach the top, an individual must know all it is possible to know about that business.

J. PAUL GETTY

A knowledge of men is the prime secret of business success.

DARIUS OGDEN MILLS

The influential man is the successful man, whether he be rich or poor.

ORISON SWETT MARDEN

Today, knowledge has power. It controls access to opportunity and advancement.

PETER F. DRUCKER

A wise man has great power, and a man of knowledge increases strength.

Bible, PROVERBS 24:5

He that has one eye is a prince among those that have none.

THOMAS FULLER

In the country of the blind, the one-eyed man is king.

MICHAEL APOSTOLIUS

As water is to flowers—so is praise to the heart of man. We thrive on being appreciated, loved and needed. When we make others feel important, and show them respect and

praise, they do their best. Nothing stimulates growth so much as praise. Whatever we praise, we increase.

Praise

We increase whatever we praise. The whole creation responds to praise, and is glad.

CHARLES FILLMORE

Appreciative words are the most powerful force for good on earth!

GEORGE W. CRANE

Good, the more communicated, more abundant grows.

JOHN MILTON

To say, "well done" to any bit of good work is to take hold of the powers which have made the effort and strengthen them beyond our knowledge!

PHILLIPS BROOKS

There is no stimulus like that which comes from the consciousness of knowing that others believe in us.

ORISON SWETT MARDEN

The deepest principle in human nature is the craving to be appreciated.

WILLIAM JAMES

It takes so little to make people happy. Just a touch, if we know how to give it, just a word fitly spoken, a slight readjustment of some bolt or pin or bearing in the delicate machinery of a soul.

FRANK CRANE

Kind words do not cost much.... Yet they accomplish much.

BLAISE PASCAL

All doors open to courtesy.

THOMAS FULLER

He that bringeth a present findeth the door open.

THOMAS FULLER

The simple act of paying positive attention to people has a great deal to do with productivity.

THOMAS J. PETERS and
ROBERT H. WATERMAN, JR.

If human beings are perceived as potentials rather than problems, as possessing strengths instead of weaknesses, as unlimited rather than dull and unresponsive, then they thrive and grow to their capabilities.

BOB CONKLIN

If you have some respect for people as they are, you can be more effective in helping them to become better than they are.

JOHN W. GARDNER

If you treat an individual...as if he were what he ought to be and could be, he will become what he ought to be and could be.

JOHANN WOLFGANG VON GOETHE

Praise invariably implies a reference to a higher standard.

ARISTOTLE

I have believed the best of every man. And find that to believe it is enough to make a bad man show him at his best, or even a good man swing his lantern higher.

WILLIAM BUTLER YEATS

Praise

I know, indeed, of nothing more subtly satisfying and cheering than a knowledge of the real good will and appreciation of others. Such happiness does not come with money, nor does it flow from a fine physical state. It cannot be bought. But it is the keenest joy, after all; and the toiler's truest and best reward.

WILLIAM DEAN HOWELLS

We are all motivated by a keen desire for praise, and the better a man is, the more he is inspired by glory. The very philosophers themselves, even in those books which they write in contempt of glory, inscribe their names.

MARCUS TULLIUS CICERO

There is no investment you can make which will pay you so well as the effort to scatter sunshine and good cheer through your establishment.

ORISON SWETT MARDEN

What sunshine is to flowers, smiles are to humanity. They are but trifles, to be sure; but, scattered along life's pathway, the good they do is inconceivable.

JOSEPH ADDISON

Few things in the world are more powerful than a positive push. A smile. A word of optimism and hope. A "you can do it" when things are tough.

RICHARD M. DeVOS

Most of us, swimming against tides of trouble the world knows nothing about, need only a bit of praise or encouragement—and we'll make the goal.

JEROME P. FLEISHMAN

Applaud us when we run,
Console us when we fall,
Cheer us when we recover....

EDMUND BURKE

266

Everything has a price.

Whatever we want in life,

we must give up something

to get it. The greater the

value, the greater the sacrifice

required. There is a high price

to pay for success. But we

must realize that the rewards of

true success are well worth the

effort. The highway to success

is a toll road.

Price

No matter what we want of life we have to give up something in order to get it.

RAYMOND HOLLIWELL

Nature cannot be tricked or cheated. She will give up to you the object of your struggles only after you have paid her price.

NAPOLEON HILL

Success is the child of drudgery and perseverance. It cannot be coaxed or bribed; pay the price and it is yours.

ORISON SWETT MARDEN

You must pay the price if you wish to secure the blessing.

ANDREW JACKSON

No one has a corner on success. It is his who pays the price.

ORISON SWETT MARDEN

This world is run with far too tight a rein for luck to interfere. Fortune sells her wares; she never gives them. In some form or other, we pay for her favors; or we go empty away.

AMELIA E. BARR

Luck is not chance—
It's toil—
Fortune's expensive smile
Is earned—

EMILY DICKINSON

Life gives nothing to man without labor.

HORACE

Labour is still, and ever will be, the inevitable price set upon everything which is valuable.

SAMUEL SMILES

Work is the open sesame of every portal, the great equalizer in the world, the true philosopher's stone which transmutes all the base metal of humanity into gold.

SIR WILLIAM OSLER

Everything you want in life has a price connected to it. There's a price to pay if you want to make things better, a price to pay just for leaving things as they are, a price for everything.

HARRY BROWNE

What keeps so many employees back is simply unwillingness to pay the price, to make the exertion, the effort to sacrifice their ease and comfort.

ORISON SWETT MARDEN

Perhaps the most valuable result of all education is the ability to make yourself do the thing you have to do, when it ought to be done, whether you like it or not. It is the first lesson that ought to be learned.

THOMAS H. HUXLEY

There is no royal road; you've got to work a good deal harder than most people want to work.

CHARLES E. WILSON

Price

Nothing worthwhile comes easily. . . . Work, continuous work and hard work, is the only way to accomplish results that last.

HAMILTON HOLT

A constant struggle, a ceaseless battle to bring success from inhospitable surroundings, is the price of all great achievements.

ORISON SWETT MARDEN

There is no victory at bargain basement prices.

DWIGHT DAVID EISENHOWER

Men talk as if victory were something fortunate. Work is victory.

RALPH WALDO EMERSON

This I do know beyond any reasonable doubt. Regardless of what you are doing, if you will pump long enough, hard enough and enthusiastically enough, sooner or later the effort will bring forth the reward.

ZIG ZIGLAR

See only that thou work and thou canst not escape the reward.

RALPH WALDO EMERSON

The one thing that matters is the effort.

ANTOINE DE SAINT-EXUPÉRY

The power to fulfill our dreams
is within each of us. We alone
have the responsibility to shape
our lives. When we understand
this, we know that nothing,
and no one, can deny us great-

ness. We are the ones pushing
ourselves forward or holding
ourselves back. The power to
succeed or fail is ours alone.

Responsibility

The day you take complete responsibility for yourself, the day you stop making any excuses, that's the day you start to the top.

O. J. SIMPSON

We have forty million reasons for failure, but not a single excuse.

RUDYARD KIPLING

Some men have thousands of reasons why they cannot do what they want to, when all they need is one reason why they can.

WILLIS R. WHITNEY

No alibi will save you from accepting the responsibility. . . .

NAPOLEON HILL

As human beings, we are endowed with freedom of choice, and we cannot shuffle off our responsibility upon the shoulders of God or nature. We must shoulder it ourselves. It is up to us.

ARNOLD J. TOYNBEE

Man must cease attributing his problems to his environment, and learn again to exercise his will—his personal responsibility. . . .

ALBERT SCHWEITZER

A man, as a general rule, owes very little to what he is born with—a man is what he makes of himself.

ALEXANDER GRAHAM BELL

I am only one,
    But still I am one.
I cannot do everything,
But still I can do something....

EDWARD EVERETT HALE

The cynic says, "One man can't do anything." I say,
"Only one man can do anything."

JOHN W. GARDNER

A man carries his success or his failure with him...it
does not depend on outside conditions....

RALPH WALDO TRINE

Not in time, place, or circumstances, but in the man
lies success....

CHARLES B. ROUSS

Not in the clamor of the crowded street,
    Not in the shouts and plaudits of the throng,
But in ourselves are triumph and defeat.

HENRY WADSWORTH LONGFELLOW

Each is responsible for his own actions.

H. L. HUNT

The ability to accept responsibility is the measure of
the man.

ROY L. SMITH

In the last analysis, the individual person is
responsible for living his own life and for "finding
himself." If he persists in shifting his responsibility to
somebody else, he fails to find out the meaning of his own
existence.

THOMAS MERTON

Responsibility

The important thing is to concentrate upon what you can do—by yourself, upon your own initiative....

HARRY BROWNE

Success on any major scale requires you to accept responsibility....In the final analysis, the one quality that all successful people have...is the ability to take on responsibility.

MICHAEL KORDA

I was taught very early that I would have to depend entirely upon myself; that my future lay in my own hands.

DARIUS OGDEN MILLS

There is a kind of elevation which does not depend on fortune; it is a certain air which distinguishes us, and seems to destine us for great things; it is a price which we imperceptibly set upon ourselves.

FRANCOIS LA ROCHEFOUCAULD

Hold yourself responsible for a higher standard than anybody else expects of you. Never excuse yourself.

HENRY WARD BEECHER

You must set the standard.

CHARLES H. KELLSTADT

You must choose the thoughts and actions that will lead you on to success....

R. C. ALLEN

You are the only one who has to live your life.

DAVID VISCOTT

obody can do it for you.

RALPH CORDINER

o one will do it for you.

BEN STEIN

one will improve your lot if you yourselves do not.

BERTOLT BRECHT

othing happens by itself....It all will come your way, once you understand that you have to make it come your way, by your own exertions.

BEN STEIN

ou have to make it happen.

JOE GREENE

ou have to do it yourself. No one else will do it for you. You must work out your own salvation.

CHARLES E. POPPLESTONE

ou might well remember that nothing can bring you success but yourself.

NAPOLEON HILL

nly you can hold yourself back, only you can stand in your own way....Only you can help yourself.

MIKHAIL STRABO

There's no one to stop you but yourself.

R. DAVID THOMAS

No one can cheat you out of ultimate success but yourselves.

RALPH WALDO EMERSON

I know that no one can really stop me but myself and that really no one can help me but myself....

PETER NIVIO ZARLENGA

More powerful than all the success slogans ever penned by human hand is the realization for every man that he has but one boss. That boss is the man—he—himself.

GABRIEL HEATTER

I guess more players lick themselves than are ever licked by an opposing team. The first thing any man has to know is how to handle himself.

CONNIE MACK

The mould of a man's fortune is in his own hands.

FRANCIS BACON

Life will always be to a large extent what we ourselves make it.

SAMUEL SMILES

Men must necessarily be the active agents of their own well-being and well-doing...they themselves must in the very nature of things be their own best helpers.

SAMUEL SMILES

We are secure to the degree that we can accept change. Security comes from being able to bend—

Security

insecurity, from breaking when things don't go our way. Those who are most secure are best able to accept change. Not by standing still, but by growing, moving, being energized, do we become secure.

Security

Security.... It's simply the recognition that changes will take place and the knowledge that you're willing to deal with whatever happens.

HARRY BROWNE

When you know that you're capable of dealing with whatever comes, you have the only security the world has to offer.

HARRY BROWNE

One has to abandon altogether the search for security, and reach out to the risk of living with both arms.... One has to court doubt and darkness as the cost of knowing. One needs a will stubborn in conflict, but apt always to total acceptance of every consequence of living and dying.

MORRIS L. WEST

Only in growth, reform, and change, paradoxically enough, is true security to be found.

ANNE MORROW LINDBERGH

Nothing is secure but life, transition, the energizing spirit.

RALPH WALDO EMERSON

Stability is not immobility.

KLEMMENS VON METTERNICH

We must be steady enough in ourselves, to be open and to let the winds of life blow through us, to be our breath, our inspiration; to breathe with them, mobile and soft in the limberness of our bodies, in our agility, our ability, as it were, to dance, and yet to stand upright....

MARY CAROLINE RICHARDS

The little reed, bending to the force of the wind, soon stood upright again when the storm had passed over.

AESOP

This tattered life is my only robe; the wind my only refuge.

MARIAN MOUNTAIN

Security depends not so much upon how much you have, as upon how much you can do without.

JOSEPH WOOD KRUTCH

The ultimate security is your understanding of reality.

H. STANLEY JUDD

It is when we all play safe that we create a world of utmost insecurity.

DAG HAMMARSKJÖLD

Playing safe is probably the most unsafe thing in the world. You cannot stand still. You must go forward....

ROBERT COLLIER

There can be no security where there is fear....

FELIX FRANKFURTER

Too many people are thinking of security instead of opportunity.

JAMES F. BYRNES

There is no security on this earth; there is only opportunity.

DOUGLAS MacARTHUR

Security

Man maintains his balance, poise, and sense of security only as he is moving forward....

MAXWELL MALTZ

We must have courage to bet on our ideas, to take the calculated risk, and to act.

MAXWELL MALTZ

Only the insecure strive for security.

WAYNE DYER

If we can learn to make uncertainty our friend....

JOHN NAISBITT

No one achieves greatness

without being of service.

Service is the essence of

greatness. All great men and

women became great because

they gave some talent or ability

in the service of others. And no

matter how small our talent,

we too can contribute in some

way to others—we too can

become great.

Service

He is great who confers the most benefits.

RALPH WALDO EMERSON

I know of no great man except those who have rendered great services to the human race.

VOLTAIRE

No man is more than another unless he does more than another.

MIGUEL DE CERVANTES

Everybody has to be somebody to somebody to be anybody.

MALCOLM S. FORBES

No person was ever honored for what he received; honor has been the reward for what he gave.

CALVIN COOLIDGE

The measure of a man is...in the number of people whom he serves.

PAUL D. MOODY

And whosoever of you will be the chiefest, shall be servant of all.

Bible, MARK 10:44

May he who is highest serve best.

ROBERT THIBODEAU

Leadership is action, not position.

DONALD H. McGANNON

Who has not served cannot command.

JOHN FLORIO

The high destiny of the individual is to serve rather than to rule....

ALBERT EINSTEIN

Our true destiny is not to be ministered unto but to minister to ourselves and to our fellow men.

FRANKLIN DELANO ROOSEVELT

For whoever exalts himself will be humbled, and whoever humbles himself will be exalted.

Bible, MATTHEW 23:12

The person who renders loyal service in a humble capacity will be chosen for higher responsibilities, just as the biblical servant who multiplied the one pound given him by his master was made ruler over ten cities....

B. C. FORBES

No man has ever risen to the real stature of spiritual manhood until he has found that it is finer to serve somebody else than it is to serve himself.

WOODROW WILSON

There is no higher religion than human service. To work for the common good is the greatest creed.

ALBERT SCHWEITZER

The highest of distinctions is service to others.

KING GEORGE VI

Service

The successful man doesn't use others, other people use the successful man, for above all the success is of service.

MARK CAINE

He is the richest man who enriches his country most; in whom the people feel richest and proudest; who gives himself with his money; who opens the doors of opportunity widest to those about him; who is ears to the deaf, eyes to the blind, and feet to the lame. Such a man makes every acre of land in his community worth more, and makes richer every man who lives near him.

ORISON SWETT MARDEN

No enterprise can exist for itself alone. It ministers to some great need, it performs some great service, not for itself, but for others; or failing therein, it ceases to be profitable and ceases to exist.

CALVIN COOLIDGE

Nothing that is weak continues to serve.

DAVID SEABURY

All business success rests on something labeled a sale, which at least momentarily weds company and customer.

THOMAS J. PETERS and
ROBERT H. WATERMAN, JR.

The golden rule for every business man is this: "Put yourself in your customer's place."

ORISON SWETT MARDEN

Right or wrong, the customer is always right.

MARSHALL FIELD

When a customer enters my store, forget me. He is king.

JOHN WANAMAKER

By understanding the simple,
we can understand the
complex. We increase our
understanding of any subject
by progressing from the simple
to the complex. When we

divide the complex into simple
parts, and master them, no
project is too difficult. The key
to mastery is simplicity.

Simplicity

I don't understand complicated problems. I only understand simple ones.

RICHARD DEUPREE

Order and simplification are the first steps toward the mastery of a subject....

THOMAS MANN

Intellectual comradeship requires that you think your thoughts through to the place where you can make the complex seem simple, the obscure quite clear.

DAVID SEABURY

Understanding reduces the greatest to simplicity, and lack of it causes the least to take on the magnitude of complexity.

RAYMOND HOLLIWELL

All great truths are simple in final analysis, and easily understood; if they are not, they are not great truths.

NAPOLEON HILL

The solutions all are simple—after you have arrived at them. But they're simple only when you know already what they are.

ROBERT M. PIRSIG

It is your work to clear away the mass of encumbering material of thought, so that you may bring into plain view the precious thing at the center of the mass.

ROBERT COLLIER

The ability to simplify means to eliminate the unnecessary so that the necessary may speak.

HANS HOFMANN

No problem can be solved until it is reduced to some simple form. The changing of a vague difficulty into a specific, concrete form is a very essential element in thinking.

JOHN J. B. MORGAN and
EWING T. WEBB

Part of my job is to train people to break down an involved question into a series of simple matters. Then we can all act intelligently.

RICHARD DEUPREE

The criterion of simplicity requires that the minimum number of assumptions be postulated.

ALBERT LOW

Less is more.

Attributed to:
LUDWIG MIES VAN DER ROHE, also
ROBERT BROWNING

The grand aim of all science is to cover the greatest number of empirical facts by logical deduction from the smallest number of hypotheses or axioms.

ALBERT EINSTEIN

All these constructions and the laws connecting them can be arrived at by the principle of looking for the mathematically simplest concepts and the link between them.

ALBERT EINSTEIN

Genius is the ability to reduce the complicated to the simple.

C. W. CERAM

Simplicity

The obvious is that which is never seen until someone expresses it simply.

KAHLIL GIBRAN

Clearness is the ornament of profound thought.

MARQUIS DE VAUVENARGUES

What is conceived well is expressed clearly....

NICOLAS BOILEAU

The most complex things are the simplest.

AGNI CELESTE

The complex develops out of the simple.

COLIN WILSON

A complex system that works is invariably found to have evolved from a simple system that works.

JOHN GALL

Every contrivance of man, every tool, every instrument, every utensil, every article designed for use, of each and every kind, evolved from very simple beginnings....

ROBERT COLLIER

It is a simple task to make things complex, but a complex task to make them simple.

MEYER'S LAW

All the great things are simple....

WINSTON CHURCHILL

Nothing is more simple than greatness; indeed, to be simple is to be great.

RALPH WALDO EMERSON

You see, God always takes the simplest way.

ALBERT EINSTEIN

Nature is an endless combination and repetition of a very few laws.

RALPH WALDO EMERSON

There is repetition everywhere, and nothing is found only once in the world.

JOHANN WOLFGANG VON GOETHE

All things have components.

J. G. GALLIMORE

Divide each difficulty into as many parts as is feasible and necessary to resolve it.

RENÉ DESCARTES

Nothing is particularly hard if you divide it into small jobs.

HENRY FORD

Complicated systems produce unexpected outcomes.

JOHN GALL

In our systems work through simplicity, consistency, and repetition.

JACK and GARRY KINDER

Simplicity

Life is really simple, but men insist on making it complicated.

CONFUCIUS

We struggle with the complexities and avoid the simplicities.

NORMAN VINCENT PEALE

Our life is frittered away by detail....Simplify, simplify.

HENRY DAVID THOREAU

See it big, and keep it simple.

WILFERD PETERSON

The wisest...keeps something of the vision of a child. Though he may think a thousand things that a child could not understand, he is always a beginner, close to the original meaning of life.

JOHN MACY

The great man is he that does not lose his child's-heart.

MENCIUS

It is the childlike mind that finds the kingdom.

CHARLES FILLMORE

Success means doing the best

we can with what we have.

Success is in the doing, not the

Success

getting—in the trying, not the

triumph. Success is a personal

standard—reaching for the

highest that is in us—becoming

all that we can be. If we do

our best, we are a success.

Success

Success, in a generally accepted sense of the term, means the opportunity to experience and to realize to the maximum the forces that are within us.

DAVID SARNOFF

Success is the maximum utilization of the ability that you have.

ZIG ZIGLAR

Every successful man I have heard of has done the best he could with conditions as he found them....

EDGAR W. HOWE

The greatest thing a man can do in this world is to make the most possible out of the stuff that has been given him. This is success, and there is no other.

ORISON SWETT MARDEN

It's what you do with what you've got.

LEROY VAN DYKE

When I am delivering my very best, then that is when I feel successful.

ART FETTIG

The measure of a man's success must be according to his ability.... The advancement he makes from the station in which he was born gives the degree of his success.

SIR WALTER BESANT

The only true measure of success is the ratio between what we might have done and what we might have been on the one hand, and the thing we have made and the thing we have made of ourselves on the other.

H. G. WELLS

Success has always been easy to measure. It is the distance between one's origins and one's final achievement....

MICHAEL KORDA

Achievement is not always success, while reputed failure often is. It is honest endeavor, persistent effort to do the best possible under any and all circumstances.

ORISON SWETT MARDEN

Life does not require us to make good; it asks only that we give our best at each level of experience.

HAROLD W. RUOPP

No matter what you do, do it to your utmost....I always attribute my success...to always requiring myself to do my level best, if only in driving a tack in straight.

RUSSELL H. CONWELL

When a man has done his best, has given his all, and in the process supplied the needs of his family and his society, that man has made a habit of succeeding.

MACK R. DOUGLAS

I do the very best I know how—the very best I can; and I mean to keep on doing so until the end.

ABRAHAM LINCOLN

I have made as much out of myself as could be made of the stuff, and no man should require more.

JEAN PAUL RICHTER

Be true to the best you know. This is your high ideal. If you do your best, you cannot do more.

H. W. DRESSER

Success

I think that at some point in your life you realize you don't have to worry if you do everything you're supposed to do right. Or if not right, if you do it the best you can...what can worry do for you? You are already doing the best you can.

JOE NAMATH

If a man has done his best, what else is there?

GEORGE S. PATTON

Whenever a man does the best he can, then that is all he can do....

HARRY S. TRUMAN

The man who has done his best has done everything.

CHARLES M. SCHWAB

It's simply a matter of doing what you do best and not worrying about what the other fellow is going to do.

JOHN R. AMOS

Success means only doing what you do well, letting someone else do the rest.

GOLDSTEIN'S TRUISM

We must do the best we can with what we have.

EDWARD ROWLAND SILL

Do what you can, with what you have, where you are.

THEODORE ROOSEVELT

Every youth owes it to himself and to the world to make the most possible out of the stuff that is in him....

ORISON SWETT MARDEN

What is possible is our highest duty.

WILLIAM E. McLAREN

To be what we are, and to become what we are capable of becoming, is the only end of life.

ROBERT LOUIS STEVENSON

I want to be all that I am capable of becoming.

KATHERINE MANSFIELD

Let each become all that he was created capable of being.

THOMAS CARLYLE

Become all that you are capable of becoming!

ROBERT J. McKAIN

Be all you can be.

Advertisement, N W AYER, Inc.

Make the most of yourself, for that is all there is of you.

RALPH WALDO EMERSON

The end of life is life. Life is action, the use of one's powers. And to use them to their height is our joy and duty. . . .

UNKNOWN

Surely a man has come to himself only when he has found the best that is in him, and has satisfied his heart with the highest achievement he is fit for.

WOODROW WILSON

Success

I dare to do all that may become a man: who dares do more is none.

WILLIAM SHAKESPEARE

I want you to start a crusade in your life—to dare to be your best.

WILLIAM DANFORTH

One of the rarest things that man ever does is to do the best he can.

JOSH BILLINGS

He who has done his best for his own time has lived for all times.

JOHANN FREDERICH VON SCHILLER

The talent of success is nothing more than doing what you can do well, and doing well whatever you do.

HENRY WADSWORTH LONGFELLOW

To try is all. It matters not if one succeeds or fails outwardly.

ROBERT THIBODEAU

Your only duty is to do the best you can.

DAVID SEABURY

Always do your best. What you plant now, you will harvest later.

OG MANDINO

To give your best is to receive the best....

RAYMOND HOLLIWELL

You must be resolutely determined that whatever you do shall always be the best of which you are capable.

CHARLES E. POPPLESTONE

There is one plain rule of life.... Try thyself unweariedly till thou findest the highest thing thou art capable of doing, faculties and outward circumstances being both duly considered, and then do it.

JOHN STUART MILL

If a man has a talent and cannot use it, he has failed. If he has a talent and uses only half of it, he has partly failed. If he has a talent and learns somehow to use the whole of it, he has gloriously succeeded, and won a satisfaction and a triumph few men ever know.

THOMAS WOLFE

The successful man is prosperous, because he has developed ninety-five percent of his ability. The failure is poor, because only five percent of his natural talents have been utilized.

CHARLES E. POPPLESTONE

I made a resolve then that I was going to amount to something if I could. And no hours, nor amount of labor, nor amount of money would deter me from giving the best that there was in me. And I have done that ever since, and I win by it. I know.

COLONEL HARLAND SANDERS

It has always been my belief that a man should do his best, regardless of how much he receives for his services, or the number of people he may be serving or the class of people served.

NAPOLEON HILL

Success

Determine to become one of the best....Sufficient money will almost automatically follow if you get to be one of the "best" in your chosen field, whatever it is.

DON G. MITCHELL

It isn't by size that you win or fail—be the best of whatever you are.

DOUGLAS MALLOCH

There is only one thing for us to do, and that is to do our level best right where we are every day of our lives; to use our best judgement, and then to trust the rest to that Power which holds the forces of the universe in His hand....

ORISON SWETT MARDEN

It is those who have this imperative demand for the best in their natures, and who will accept nothing short of it, that hold the banners of progress, that set the standards, the ideals, for others.

ORISON SWETT MARDEN

To have known the best, and to have known it for the best, is success in life.

JOHN W. MacKAY

We do not do well except when we know where the best is and when we are assured that we have touched it and hold its power within us.

JOSEPH JOUBERT

When a man feels throbbing within him the power to do what he undertakes as well as it can possibly be done, and all of his faculties say "amen" to what he is doing, and give their unqualified approval to his efforts,—this is happiness, this is success.

ORISON SWETT MARDEN

A change in what we tell
ourselves will result in a
change in our behavior.
Positive, repetitive self-talk
changes our self-image. And

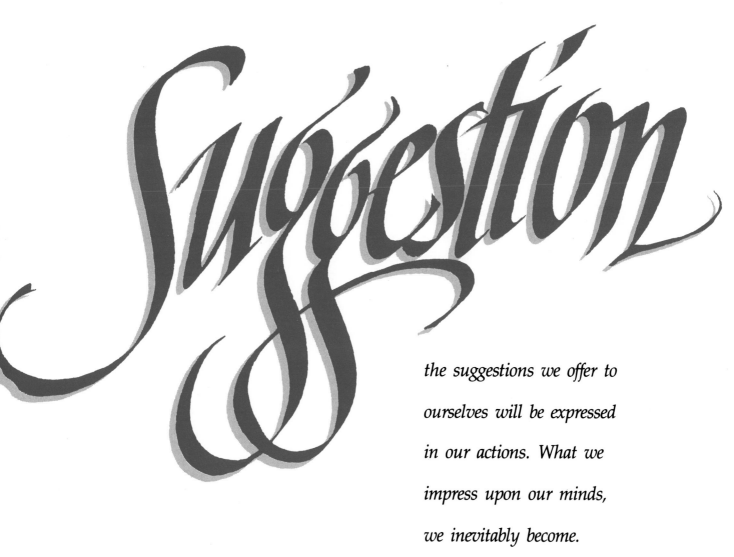

the suggestions we offer to
ourselves will be expressed
in our actions. What we
impress upon our minds,
we inevitably become.

Suggestion

We all have voices in our heads which talk to us on an almost constant basis. Our voices give us messages continually, and what they say to us affects us....

JULIENE BERK

Every waking moment we talk to ourselves about the things we experience. Our self-talk, the thoughts we communicate to ourselves, in turn control the way we feel and act.

JOHN LEMBO

This inner speech, your thoughts, can cause you to be rich or poor, loved or unloved, happy or unhappy, attractive or unattractive, powerful or weak....

RALPH CHARELL

The "self-image" is the key to human personality and human behavior. Change the self image and you change the personality and the behavior.

MAXWELL MALTZ

Relentless, repetitive self talk is what changes our self image.

DENIS E. WAITLEY

Realizing that our actions, feelings and behavior are the result of our own images and beliefs gives us the lever that psychology has always needed for changing personality.

MAXWELL MALTZ

All causes are essentially mental, and whosoever comes into daily contact with a high order of thinking must take on some of it.

CHARLES FILLMORE

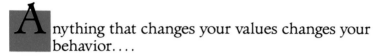

Anything that changes your values changes your behavior....

GEORGE SHEEHAN

To begin with, you must realize that any idea accepted by the brain is automatically transformed into an action of some sort. It may take seconds or minutes or longer—but ideas always produce a reaction of some sort.

SCOTT REED

Every suggested idea produces a corresponding physical reaction....Every idea constantly repeated ends by being engraved upon the brain, provoking the act which corresponds to that idea.

SCOTT REED

Information storage has to take place at the unconscious level.

PAUL G. THOMAS

The subjective mind is entirely under the control of the objective mind. With the utmost fidelity it reproduces and works out to its final consequences whatever the objective mind impresses upon it....

THOMAS TROWARD

It is a psychological law that whatever we desire to accomplish we must impress upon the subjective or subconscious mind....

ORISON SWETT MARDEN

We must realize that the subconscious mind is the law of action and always expresses what the conscious mind has impressed on it. What we regularly entertain in our mind creates a conception of self. What we conceive ourselves to be, we become.

GRACE SPEARE

Suggestion

Your self image is your pattern!....Every thought has an activity visualized. Every activity belongs to a pattern. You identify with your pattern or thought. Your pattern leads your life.

J. G. GALLIMORE

Any idea, plan, or purpose may be placed in the mind through repetition of thought.

NAPOLEON HILL

Whatever we plant in our subconscious mind and nourish with repetition and emotion will one day become a reality.

EARL NIGHTINGALE

You affect your subconscious mind by verbal repetition.

W. CLEMENT STONE

Only one thing registers on the subconscious mind: repetitive application—practice. What you practice is what you manifest.

GRACE SPEARE

Repeat anything often enough and it will start to become you.

TOM HOPKINS

One comes to believe whatever one repeats to oneself sufficiently often, whether the statement be true or false. It comes to be the dominating thought in one's mind.

ROBERT COLLIER

Any thought that is passed on to the subconscious often enough and convincingly enough is finally accepted....

ROBERT COLLIER

These repetitive words and phrases...are merely methods of convincing the subconscious mind....

CLAUDE M. BRISTOL

Constant repetition carries conviction....

ROBERT COLLIER

You will be a failure, until you impress the subconscious with the conviction you are a success. This is done by making an affirmation which "clicks."

FLORENCE SCOVEL SHINN

It's the repetition of...affirmations that leads to belief. And once that belief becomes a deep conviction, things begin to happen.

CLAUDE M. BRISTOL

As long as you know what it is you desire, then by simply affirming that it is yours—firmly and positively, with no ifs, buts, or maybes—over and over again, from the minute you arise in the morning until the time you go to sleep at night, and as many times during the day as your work or activities permit, you will be drawn to those people, places, and events that will bring your desires to you.

SCOTT REED

The whole idea...is to enable you to see mentally the picture at all hours of the day.

CLAUDE M. BRISTOL

Suggestion

No flame of desire can long continue to burn vigorously if its supply of suggestive fuel be cut off from it.

ROBERT COLLIER

Your ability to use the principle of autosuggestion will depend, very largely, upon your capacity to concentrate upon a given desire until that desire becomes a burning obsession.

NAPOLEON HILL

You must intensify and render continuous by repeatedly presenting with suggestive ideas and mental pictures of the feast of good things, and the flowing fountain, which awaits the successful achievement or attainment of the desires.

ROBERT COLLIER

You must begin to think of yourself as becoming the person you want to be.

DAVID VISCOTT

We cannot always control our thoughts, but we can control our words, and repetition impresses the subconscious, and we are then master of the situation.

FLORENCE SCOVEL SHINN

Self-suggestion makes you master of yourself.

W. CLEMENT STONE

Time can't be managed. But what can be managed are our activities and how we "spend" time. And all

Time Management

the experts agree: managing our activities begins with planning. So by knowing what's important for us—planning our work and working our plan—we become wise managers.

Time Management

To choose time is to save time.

FRANCIS BACON

Time has no meaning in itself unless we choose to give it significance.

LEO BUSCAGLIA

Don't serve time, make time serve you.

WILLIE SUTTON

We always have time enough, if we will but use it aright.

JOHANN WOLFGANG VON GOETHE

We realize our dilemma goes deeper than shortage of time; it is basically a problem of priorities....We confess...."We have left undone those things that we ought to have done; and we have done those things which we ought not to have done."

CHARLES E. HUMMELL

We have left undone those things which we ought to have done; and we have done those things which we ought not to have done.

THE BOOK OF COMMON PRAYER

Set priorities for your goals....A major part of successful living lies in the ability to put first things first. Indeed, the reason most major goals are not achieved is that we spend our time doing second things first.

ROBERT J. McKAIN

We need....A sense of the value of time—that is, of the best way to divide one's time into one's various activities....

ARNOLD BENNETT

Concentrating on the essentials...we will then be accomplishing the greatest possible results with the effort expended.

TED W. ENGSTROM and
R. ALEC MacKENZIE

All time management begins with planning.

TOM GREENING and DICK HOBSON

In all planning you make a list and you set priorities.

ALAN LAKEIN

Review our priorities, ask the question: What's the best use of our time right now?

ALAN LAKEIN

The key to setting priorities, the order in which you must accomplish things, is to ask yourself, "What is my payoff in doing this activity? How does this fit in with my long-term objectives...?"

SUCCESS MAGAZINE

Is what I'm doing or about to do getting us closer to our objective?

ROBERT TOWNSEND

Management manages by making decisions and by seeing that those decisions are implemented.

HAROLD S. GENEEN

The idea is to make decisions and act on them—to decide what is important to accomplish, to decide how something can best be accomplished, to find time to work at it and to get it done.

KAREN KAKASCIK

Time Management

Anything that is wasted effort represents wasted time. The best management of our time thus becomes linked inseparably with the best utilization of our efforts.

TED W. ENGSTROM and
R. ALEC MacKENZIE

What do you want to get done?....
In what order of importance?....
Over what period of time?....
What is the time available?....
What is the best strategy for application of time to projects for the most effective results?

TED W. ENGSTROM and
R. ALEC MacKENZIE

Plan your work for today and every day, then work your plan.

NORMAN VINCENT PEALE

He who every morning plans the transactions of the day and follows out that plan, carries a thread that will guide him through the labyrinth of the most busy life.

VICTOR HUGO

Write down the most important things you have to do tomorrow. Now, number them in the order of their true importance. The first thing tomorrow morning, start working on item Number 1, and stay with it until completed. Then take item Number 2 the same way. Then Number 3, and so on. Don't worry if you don't complete everything on the schedule. At least you will have completed the most important projects before getting to the less important ones.

IVY LEE

Make time for getting big tasks done every day. Plan your daily work load in advance. Single out the relatively few small jobs that absolutely must be done immediately in the morning. Then go directly to the big tasks, try to pursue them to completion.

BOARDROOM REPORTS

Truth is what is. Truth is neither good nor bad, ugly nor beautiful. Truth is just what exists—it is reality. The successful are realists.

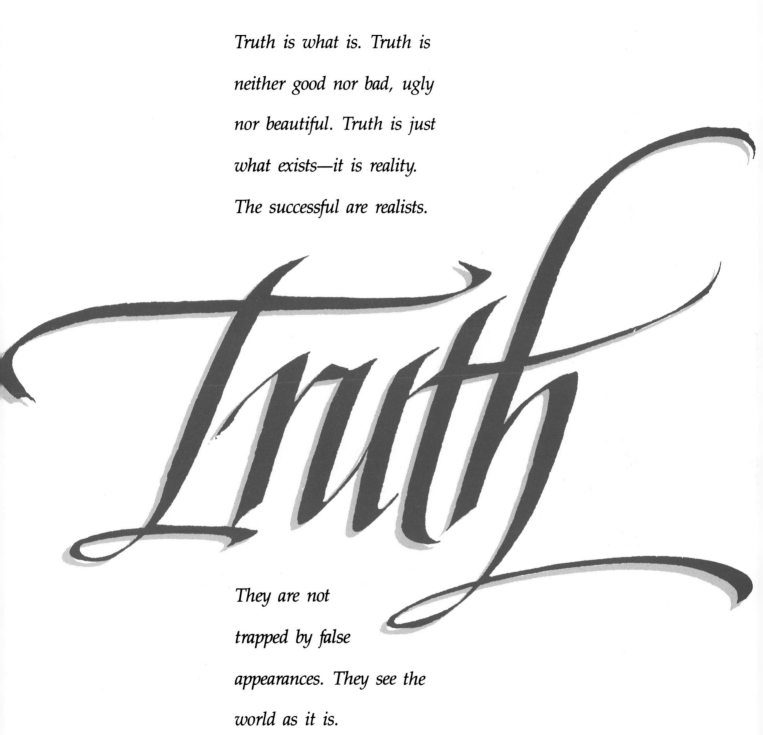

They are not trapped by false appearances. They see the world as it is.

Truth

What is, is.

WERNER ERHARD

Truth is exact correspondence with reality.

PARAMAHANSA YOGANANDA

Truth is reality.

MARY CAROLINE RICHARDS

Reality is what is.

J. KRISHNAMURTI

What is, is; and what ain't, ain't.

JOSEPH E. GRANVILLE

The truth simply is that's all. It doesn't need reasons: it doesn't have to be right: it's just the truth. Period.

CARL FREDERICK

Effective thinking consists of being able to arrive at the truth; truth being defined as that which exists.

CALVIN S. HALL

The basic truth of all things, as nearly as we may ever dream of determining and knowing this truth, is form, that which is, as it is. The way and shape of the thing no less than the thing itself.

WILLIAM SAROYAN

Things are as they are....Looking out into it [the universe] at night, we make no comparisons between right and wrong stars, nor between well and badly arranged constellations.

ALAN W. WATTS

Truth is not beautiful, neither is it ugly. Why should it be either? Truth is truth....

OWEN C. MIDDLETON

Reality is neither good nor bad; it just is.

ARBIE M. DALE

In nature, the emphasis is in what is rather than what ought to be.

HUSTON SMITH

It has sometimes been said that we find nowhere in nature an analogue of the difference between "happens" and "is," on the one hand, and "ought," on the other hand.

WOLFGANG KÖHLER

Reality isn't the way you wish things to be, nor the way they appear to be, but the way they actually are.

ROBERT J. RINGER

What is a lie? It is to say what is real is not real. It is to deny the existence of what exists.

PETER NIVIO ZARLENGA

All necessary truth is its own evidence.

RALPH WALDO EMERSON

Everything is self-evident.

RENÉ DESCARTES

The fundamental laws are in the long run merely statements that every event is itself and not some different event.

C. S. LEWIS

 Truth

or everything exists and not one sigh nor smile nor tear, one hair nor particle of dust, not one can pass away.

WILLIAM BLAKE

A blade of grass is always a blade of grass, whether in one country or another.

SAMUEL JOHNSON

Meaning and reality were not hidden somewhere behind things, they were in them, in all of them.

HERMANN HESSE

There is, so I believe, in the essence of everything, something that we cannot call learning. There is, my friend, only a knowledge—that is everywhere....

HERMANN HESSE

Theories are private property, but truth is common stock.

CHARLES CALEB COLTON

There's nothing you can know that isn't known.

JOHN LENNON and
PAUL McCARTNEY

I know now that there is no one thing that is true—it is all true.

Attributed to ERNEST HEMINGWAY

This is all there is.

ALAN W. WATTS

One universe made up of all that is; and one God in it all, and one principle of being, and one law, the reason shared by all thinking creatures, and one truth.

MARCUS AURELIUS

The truth has a million faces, but there is only one truth.

HERMANN HESSE

Truth has no special time of its own. Its hour is now—always.

ALBERT SCHWEITZER

Nature....She pardons no mistakes. Her yea is yea, and her nay, nay.

RALPH WALDO EMERSON

Nature understands no jesting. She is always true, always serious, always severe. She is always right, and the errors are always those of man.

JOHANN WOLFGANG VON GOETHE

Truth does not contradict truth.

ELIZER ZVI ZWEIFEL

Nature never deceives us; it is we who deceive ourselves.

JEAN JACQUES ROUSSEAU

I see that the elementary laws never apologize....

WALT WHITMAN

If we all worked on the assumption that what is accepted as true is really true, there would be little hope of advance.

ORVILLE WRIGHT

If fifty million people say a foolish thing, it is still a foolish thing.

BERTRAND RUSSELL

Wrong is wrong, no matter who does it or who says it.

MALCOLM X

What is true is true, and what is false is false....

EMANUEL SWEDENBORG

An idea isn't responsible for the people who believe in it.

DON MARQUIS

The fact that an opinion has been widely held is no evidence whatever that it is not utterly absurd....

BERTRAND RUSSELL

No matter what you believe, it doesn't change the facts.

AL KERSHA

Facts do not cease to exist because they are ignored.

ALDOUS HUXLEY

Truth does not change because it is, or is not, believed by a majority of the people.

GIORDANO BRUNO

The sky is not less blue because the blind man does not see it.

DANISH PROVERB

General principles are not the less true or important because from their nature they elude immediate observation; they are like the air, which is not the less necessary because we neither see nor feel it.

WILLIAM HAZLITT

The god whom science recognizes must be a God of universal laws exclusively, a God who does a wholesale, not a retail business. He cannot accommodate his processes to the convenience of individuals.

WILLIAM JAMES

It may be said with a degree of assurance that not everything that meets the eye is as it appears.

ROD SERLING

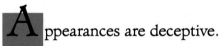Appearances are deceptive.

AESOP

Things are not always what they seem; the first appearance deceives many: the intelligence of a few perceives what has been carefully hidden....

PHAEDRUS

How little do they see what is, who frame their judgements upon that which seems.

ROBERT SOUTHEY

You and I do not see things as they are. We see things as we are.

HERB COHEN

We are all captives of the pictures in our head—our belief that the world we have experienced is the world that really exists.

WALTER LIPPMANN

Truth is not a matter of personal viewpoint.

VERNON HOWARD

Learn to see things as they really are, not as we imagine they are.

VERNON HOWARD

See it like it is!

HERB COHEN

Our job is only to hold up the mirror—to tell and show the public what has happened....

WALTER CRONKITE

And that's the way it is....

WALTER CRONKITE

This is the way things are.... They are the way they are!

THOMAS WOLFE

More wisdom is latent in things-as-they-are than in all the words men use.

ANTOINE DE SAINT-EXUPÉRY

One might speak to great length of the three corners of reality—what was seen, what was thought to be seen, and what was thought ought to be seen.

MARVIN BELL

Truth will always be truth, regardless of lack of understanding, disbelief or ignorance.

W. CLEMENT STONE

The facts, if they are there, speak for themselves.

DAVID SEABURY

There is no need to seek truth; only stop having views.

SENGSTAN

There is an abiding beauty which may be appreciated by those who will see things as they are and who will ask for no reward except to see.

VERA BRITTAIN

We must have strong minds, ready to accept facts as they are....

HARRY S. TRUMAN

Things are more like they are now than they have ever been before.

DWIGHT D. EISENHOWER

The facts are always friendly...every bit of evidence one can acquire, in any area, leads one that much closer to what is true.

CARL ROGERS

We must learn to tailor our concepts to fit reality, instead of trying to stuff reality into our concepts.

VICTOR DANIELS and
LAURENCE J. HOROWITZ

Truth

Are you going out after the truth, or are you going out after something you believe?

RICHARD ROSE

Sit down before fact like a little child, and be prepared to give up every preconceived notion, follow humbly wherever and to whatever abyss Nature leads, or you shall learn nothing.

THOMAS H. HUXLEY

For here we are not afraid to follow truth wherever it may lead....

THOMAS JEFFERSON

No authority is higher than reality.

PETER NIVIO ZARLENGA

The successful people of this world take life as it comes....They just go out and deal with the world as it is.

BEN STEIN

We have understanding to

the degree that we see

Understanding

how things change. Seeing

the flow of events and how

history develops, gives us

understanding. Seeing what

has gone before gives insight

into what may be.

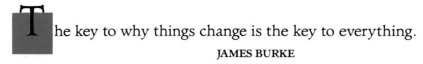

Understanding

The key to why things change is the key to everything.

JAMES BURKE

We can chart our future clearly and wisely only when we know the path which has led to the present.

ADLAI STEVENSON

The present contains nothing more than the past, and what is found in the effect was already in the cause.

HENRI BERGSON

Return to the root and you will find the meaning....

SENGSTAN

The farther backward you can look, the farther forward you are likely to see.

WINSTON CHURCHILL

If you want to understand today, you have to search yesterday.

PEARL S. BUCK

Life...can only be understood backwards....

SÖREN KIERKEGAARD

When I want to understand what is happening today or try to decide what will happen tomorrow, I look back.

OLIVER WENDELL HOLMES, JR.

Time is the wisest counsellor.

PERICLES

Vision is the gift of seeing
clearly what may be. Vision
expands our horizons. The
more we see, the more we
can achieve; the
grander our

Vision

vision, the more glorious our
accomplishment. The courage
to follow our dreams is the
first step toward destiny.

Vision

Nothing happens unless first a dream.

CARL SANDBURG

All men who have achieved great things have been dreamers.

ORISON SWETT MARDEN

We grow great by dreams. All big men are dreamers.

WOODROW WILSON

I have heard it said that the first ingredient of success—the earliest spark in the dreaming youth— is this: dream a great dream.

JOHN ALAN APPLEMAN

Our first journey is to find that special place for us....

EARL NIGHTINGALE

I always have to dream up there against the stars. If I don't dream I'll make it, I won't even get close.

HENRY J. KAISER

It may be those who do most, dream most.

STEPHEN LEACOCK

The more you can dream, the more you can do.

MICHAEL KORDA

High achievement always takes place in the framework of high expectation.

JACK and GARRY KINDER

Big thinking precedes big achievement.

WILFERD A. PETERSON

You have to think big to be big.

CLAUDE M. BRISTOL

Think little goals and expect little achievements. Think big goals and win big success.

DAVID JOSEPH SCHWARTZ

I was once asked if a big business man ever reached his objective. I replied that if a man ever reached his objective he was not a big business man.

CHARLES M. SCHWAB

To desire is to obtain; to aspire is to achieve.

JAMES ALLEN

Our aspirations are our possibilities.

ROBERT BROWNING

You will become as small as your controlling desire; or as great as your dominant aspiration.

JAMES ALLEN

Only things the dreamers make live on. They are the eternal conquerors.

HERBERT KAUFMAN

Vision....It reaches beyond the thing that is, into the conception of what can be. Imagination gives you the picture. Vision gives you the impulse to make the picture your own.

ROBERT COLLIER

Vision

We lift ourselves by our thought, we climb upon our vision of ourselves. If you want to enlarge your life, you must first enlarge your thought of it and of yourself. Hold the ideal of yourself as you long to be, always, everywhere—your ideal of what you long to attain—the ideal of health, efficiency, success.

ORISON SWETT MARDEN

The size of your accomplishments, the quality of your achievement, will depend very largely on how big a man you see in yourself, what sort of image you get of your possible self, yourself at your best.

ORISON SWETT MARDEN

Man cannot aspire if he look down; if he rise, he must look up.

SAMUEL SMILES

We cannot rise higher than our thought of ourselves.

ORISON SWETT MARDEN

If a man constantly aspires is he not elevated?

HENRY DAVID THOREAU

I have seen gleams in the face and eyes of the man that have let you look into a higher country.

THOMAS CARLYLE

The cities and mansions that people dream of are those in which they finally live....

LEWIS MUMFORD

The empires of the future are empires of the mind.

WINSTON CHURCHILL

Where there is no vision, the people perish....

Bible, PROVERBS 29:18

When you cease to dream you cease to live.

MALCOLM S. FORBES

I believe that any single dream contains the essential message about our existence.

FREDERICK S. PERLS

Makers of empire, they have fought for bigger things than crowns and higher seats than thrones.

HERBERT KAUFMAN

The idea for which this nation stands will not survive if the highest goal free man can set themselves is an amiable mediocrity....Excellence implies....Striving for the highest standards in every phase of life.

JOHN W. GARDNER

No vision and you perish;
No ideal, and you're lost;
Your heart must ever cherish
Some faith at any cost.

Some hope, some dream to cling to,
Some rainbow in the sky,
Some melody to sing to,
Some service that is high.

HARRIET DU AUTERMONT

To come to be you must have a vision of Being, a Dream, a Purpose, a Principle. You will become what your vision is....

PETER NIVIO ZARLENGA

We go where our vision is.

JOSEPH MURPHY

Vision

The only limits are, as always, those of vision.

JAMES BROUGHTON

Cherish your visions and your dreams as they are the children of your soul; the blue prints of your ultimate achievements.

NAPOLEON HILL

If one advances confidently in the direction of his dreams, and endeavors to live the life which he has imagined, he will meet with a success unexpected in common hours.

HENRY DAVID THOREAU

Dream lofty dreams, and as you dream, so shall you become. Your vision is the promise of what you shall one day be; your ideal is the prophecy of what you shall at last unveil.

JAMES ALLEN

All who have accomplished great things have had a great aim, have fixed their gaze on a goal which was high, one which sometimes seemed impossible....

ORISON SWETT MARDEN

The only way to discover the limits of the possible is to go beyond them into the impossible.

ARTHUR C. CLARKE

You see things; and you say, "Why?" But I dream things that never were; and I say, "Why not?"

GEORGE BERNARD SHAW

Dream manfully and nobly, and thy dreams shall be prophets.

EDWARD ROBERT BULWER-LYTTON

man's dreams are an index to his greatness.

ZADOK RABINOWITZ

n the long run, men hit only what they aim at. Therefore...they had better aim at something high.

HENRY DAVID THOREAU

im for the highest....

ANDREW CARNEGIE

oo low they build, who build beneath the stars.

EDWARD YOUNG

deals are like stars; you will not succeed in reaching them with your hands. But like the seafaring man on the desert of waters, you choose them as your guides, and following them you will reach your destiny.

CARL SCHURZ

ar away there in the sunshine are my highest aspirations. I may not reach them, but I can look up and see their beauty, believe in them, and try to follow where they lead.

LOUISA MAY ALCOTT

A man's reach should exceed his grasp....

ROBERT BROWNING

It is the ultimate wisdom of the mountains that a man is never more a man than when he is striving for what is beyond his grasp.

JAMES RAMSEY ULLMAN

The hand cannot reach higher than does the heart.

ORISON SWETT MARDEN

Vision

Dream no small dreams for they have no power to move the hearts of men.

JOHANN WOLFGANG VON GOETHE

Dwell in thought upon the Grandest,
And the Grandest you shall see;
Fix your mind upon the Highest,
And the Highest you shall be.

UNKNOWN

Man's mind stretched to a new idea never goes back to its original dimensions.

OLIVER WENDELL HOLMES

You are the one who can stretch your own horizon....

EDGAR F. MAGNIN

Dreams show you that you have the power....

HELEN SCHUCMAN and
WILLIAM THETFORD

We've got to have a dream if we are going to make a dream come true.

DENIS E. WAITLEY

If you don't have a dream, how are you going to make a dream come true?

OSCAR HAMMERSTEIN II,
South Pacific

Man, alone, has the power to transform his thoughts into physical reality; man, alone, can dream and make his dreams come true.

NAPOLEON HILL

Wisdom comes from the experience of living. To travel the road of wisdom requires knowledge of ourselves and others—in love and hatred, in

joy and sorrow, in victory and defeat. To experience life, and to learn its truth—this is wisdom.

Wisdom

Wisdom is meaningless until our own experience has given it meaning.

BERGEN EVANS

There are many truths of which the full meaning cannot be realized until personal experience has brought it home.

JOHN STUART MILL

Practical wisdom is only to be learned in the school of experience. Precepts and instructions are useful so far as they go, but, without the discipline of real life, they remain of the nature of theory only.

SAMUEL SMILES

You know more of a road by having travelled it than by all the conjectures and descriptions in the world.

WILLIAM HAZLITT

Let no one be deluded that a knowledge of the path can substitute for putting one foot in front of the other.

MARY CAROLINE RICHARDS

Wisdom and understanding can only become the possession of individual men by travelling the old road of observation, attention, perseverance, and industry.

SAMUEL SMILES

What is the price of experience? Do men buy it for a song? Or wisdom for a dance in the street? No, it is bought with the price of all that a man hath, his house, his wife, his children.

WILLIAM BLAKE

The ear that heareth the reproof of life abideth among the wise.

Bible, PROVERBS 15:31

I have known it for a long time but I have only just experienced it. Now I know it not only with my intellect, but with my eyes, with my heart, with my stomach.

HERMANN HESSE

Wisdom is found only in truth.

JOHANN WOLFGANG VON GOETHE

The truth is lived, not taught.

HERMANN HESSE

Life is a succession of lessons which must be lived to be understood.

RALPH WALDO EMERSON

If we live truly, we shall see truly.

RALPH WALDO EMERSON

Do the thing you know, and you shall learn the truth you need to know.

GEORGE MacDONALD

I hear and I forget. I see and I remember. I do and I understand.

CHINESE PROVERB

Knowledge conquered by labour becomes a possession—a property entirely our own.

SAMUEL SMILES

Wisdom

Wisdom is knowledge which has become a part of one's being....

ORISON SWETT MARDEN

Time ripens all things; no man is born wise.

MIGUEL DE CERVANTES

Knowledge comes but wisdom lingers.

ALFRED LORD TENNYSON

Knowledge comes, but wisdom lingers. It may not be difficult to store up in the mind a vast quantity of facts within a comparatively short time, but the ability to form judgements requires the severe discipline of hard work and the tempering heat of experience and maturity.

CALVIN COOLIDGE

The words printed here are concepts. You must go through the experiences.

CARL FREDERICK

The experience gathered from books, though often valuable, is but the nature of learning: whereas the experience gained from actual life is of the nature of wisdom....

SAMUEL SMILES

Knowledge can be communicated, but wisdom cannot. A man can find it, he can live it, he can be filled and sustained by it, but he cannot utter or teach it.

HERMANN HESSE

Wisdom is perishable. Unlike information or knowledge, it cannot be stored in a computer or recorded in a book. It expires with each passing generation.

SID TAYLOR

The universe is one great kindergarten for man. Everything that exists has brought with it its own peculiar lesson. The mountain teaches stability and grandeur; the ocean immensity and change. Forests, lakes, and rivers, clouds and winds, stars and flowers, stupendous glaciers and crystal snowflakes,—every form of animate or inanimate existence, leaves its impress upon the soul of man. Even the bee and ant have brought their little lessons of industry and economy.

ORISON SWETT MARDEN

Who is a wise man? He who learns of all men.

The TALMUD

If you wish to know the road up the mountain, ask the man who goes back and forth on it.

ZENRIN

He that walketh with wise men shall be wise....

Bible, PROVERBS 13:20

Follow then the shining ones, the wise, the awakened, the loving, for they know how to work and forbear.

GAUTAMA BUDDHA

Blessed is the man who finds wisdom, the man who gains understanding, for she is more profitable than silver and yields better returns than gold. She is more precious than rubies; nothing you desire can compare with her.

Bible, PROVERBS 3:13-15